MAKING MEETINGS MATTER

How Smart Leaders
Orchestrate Powerful Conversations
in the Digital Age *4|10|16*

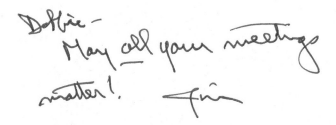

*Debbie —
May all your meetings
matter!   Jim*

James Ware, PhD

INDIE BOOKS
INTERNATIONAL

ISBN-10: 1-941870-48-1
ISBN-13: 978-1-941870-48-8
LOC: 2015959784

Designed by Joni McPherson, mcphersongraphics.com

INDIE BOOKS INTERNATIONAL, LLC
2424 VISTA WAY, SUITE 316
OCEANSIDE, CA 92054
www.indiebooksintl.com

PRAISE FOR MAKING MEETINGS MATTER

"The pace of change in the workplace is blistering. At the heart of the transformation is a massive shift in the way people interact while working. The insights shared in this book are critical for understanding these changes. I highly recommend this book to anyone interested in better understanding the workplace of the future."

Mike Wagner, Chief Executive Officer, Kimball Office

"Jim Ware has done the impossible; he actually makes meetings relevant and, dare I say it, even fun again. Don't waste another minute on ineffective meetings now that you've learned the secret to changing the conversation."

Ruth Ross, Engagement Evangelist, speaker and author of *Coming Alive: The Journey To Reengage Your Life And Career*

"Jim Ware is a leading thinker and innovator in the space of organization and work productivity. This book offers insightful new ideas and practical tools to help individuals, teams, and ultimately organizations become more efficient and effective. I highly recommend it."

Mike Dulworth, President and CEO, Executive Networks, and author of *The Connect Effect*

"The best toolset we have discovered to recover time for innovative and collaborative thinking by our staff is the meeting mindset presented in this wonderful book. I highly recommend that you and your staff engage with this book as soon as possible."

Mike Moss, Chief Executive Officer, Society of College and University Planners

"Jim Ware's new book is the definitive guide for managers who want to learn how to transform meetings from time-wasters into

powerful resources for creating extraordinary engagement and high performance. Read this book and discover how you can leverage the collective wisdom of your colleagues to succeed in today's rapidly changing and complex world."

Rod Collins, author of *Wiki Management* and *Leadership in a Wiki World*

"We've all had the experience of being horribly bored (and resentful of the waste of time) as meetings droned on and on. In his latest book, and in the clearest language, Jim Ware has laid out the primary key to change all that: he calls it having a conversation."

Judith M. Bardwick, PhD, author of *Danger in the Comfort Zone, In Praise of Good Business, One Foot out the Door*

"Meetings are at the heart of organizational work. Yet very few organizational leaders know how to run meetings effectively, or even how to participate in them. Jim Ware has produced a compelling analysis of why – and how – we must reinvent leadership for the digital age."

Mike Johnson, Founder and Executive Chair, FutureWork Forum, and author of *The Worldwide Workplace: Solving the Global Talent Equation*

"This book details step-by-step the new rules, tools, and easy approaches for having great and productive meetings. Get this wonderful book now and be the change you wish to see!"

Bill Jensen, author of *Simplicity and Future Strong*

"Jim Ware has taken the subject of meetings, exploded it, and put it back together, not as a routine and obligatory process, but as a source of inspiration and inventiveness."

Chris Hood, Managing Director, CBRE GCS Occupancy Services

"Jim Ware has presented an enjoyable-to-read, easy-to-understand book that dissects the meeting process into implementable steps that help leaders achieve their goals. A must-read for those who want to be effective leaders."

Bary Sherman, CEO, PEP Worldwide-USA

"I have read and studied hundreds of references on the subject of effective meetings, but nothing that compares to the insights and perspectives presented in Making Meetings Matter. This book is a must-read for all leaders to maximize the engagement and performance of their most valuable asset: people."

Kent Reyling, Director of Market Education, Kimball Office

"An easy read. That's a good thing, because this book is so full of usable information that you will want to refer to it over and over again!"

Dr. Patt Schwab, CSP, founder of FUNdamentally Speaking

TABLE OF CONTENTS

FOREWORD

The nature of conversation and communication has changed dramatically. We find ourselves communicating faster, more frequently, over greater distances, and with many more people. Yet we seem to be less effective.

Why is that so? Because of technology every business is now doing business globally; there are almost no meaningful geographic boundaries any more. Yes, there are still a few basically local businesses—the barbershop, the nail salon, the local farmers market. But almost everybody else is now doing business regionally, nationally, and internationally.

We are also starting up businesses at a much faster rate. There is an expectation that a business can go from startup to scale-up in a much shorter period of time.

What that really means is that organizations must build consensus and make decisions rapidly. When we think about meetings and how central they are to doing business in this global economy, we must align individual ideas and reach group decisions much more quickly than we have in the past. If we don't our competitors will beat us in the marketplace.

And yet the habits and patterns we have developed about verbal dialogue are still stuck somewhere in the 1950s, 1960s and/or 1970s. We've made all kinds of advances in the way we communicate with written words. We can e-mail, we can text, we can tweet; we've figured out how to do that with fewer words and characters, and with much more alacrity.

However, even with those advances we aren't producing the level of understanding and agreement that our organizations need to be agile and effective. One senior executive I know recently told me he believes the biggest challenge his organization faces is not its competitors but the fact that his strategic vision is not well-understood within the company. On questioning he admitted that he had been unable to spread the strategic vision and related action imperatives that were formulated in the board room throughout the organization.

In fact, every single senior executive I've spoken with in the last year has admitted to me that they struggle to cascade their visions, priorities, and Key Performance Indicators (KPIs) throughout the organization. They know it's important; they just can't make it happen.

Aligning people and their efforts across organizational units, time zones, and continents remains the biggest challenge that senior executives face, in spite of all that wonderful technology we have access to. Being connected technically is only the beginning; connecting people's hearts and minds is another matter altogether.

My clients tell me that the power of the One Page Business Plan® is that it aligns ideas and helps to change behaviors quickly and clearly.

When I developed the One Page Business Plan® over twenty-five years ago my goal was to create that alignment and achieve those connections from one organizational unit to another. But the one-page plan succeeds best when it is accompanied by conversations that produce deep understanding of what those strategies and those KPIs mean on a day-to-day basis.

In my experience most organizational conversations are woefully inadequate at achieving that goal.

We need to bring business meetings into the digital age in the same way that we have reinvented business planning and written communication. The current form of corporate meetings is bent and broken; it just doesn't fit the realities of the global, technology-rich world that we live in today.

This book is all about reinventing the business meeting. It offers advice and guidance for streamlining and strengthening all kinds of corporate conversations; but it focuses where it should, on the formal meetings that fill up over 50 percent of most managers' calendars.

When the meetings I'm involved in are winding up, I like to ask the participants a simple question: "What if anything will you do differently as a result of the time we've spent together?" It's a powerful way for me to learn whether I've been heard or understood.

I challenge you to ask that same question at the end of every meeting you participate in, and ask it of this book as well. What if anything will you do differently as a result of reading this book?

My deepest hope is that you will approach all your meetings from now on with a fresh perspective, with respect for the other participants, and with genuine curiosity about what insights and decisions the meeting will generate that could not have happened any other way. That's the way to make your meetings matter.

Jim Horan
Founder and CEO
The One Page Business Plan® Company
November, 2015

INTRODUCTION

Thank you for picking up *Making Meetings Matter*. If you are like most of us, you spend way too much time in bad meetings and other conversations at work that go nowhere.

How long has it been since you were in a meeting you felt was totally unproductive? Have you ever wished you had a Star Trek pocket communicator you could command to "Beam me up, Scotty" just to get away from yet another meaningless meeting? How long has it been since you *led* a meeting like that?

Be honest; it's happened to every one of us.

Do you spend time in meetings thinking about the "real work" you are not getting done, or holding your smartphone in your lap and sneaking a peek at your e-mail inbox to see what's going on out there in the real world? Or have you ever sent a surreptitious text asking a colleague to call you out of a meeting for some fake crisis or phone call from a "client" that just can't wait?

Well, I've got a simple message for you: *it doesn't have to be that way.*

This book is dedicated to the proposition that meetings can be meaningful, productive, and even fun—all at the same time.

Here's why that is so important.

Not only has the world changed in the last twenty years, but the nature of work itself has changed too. Yet many organizations are still operating as if their employees just came from the farm to the city and need to be told what to do as they take their place on the assembly line. We're still applying nineteenth-century industrial-age management practices in a twenty-first-century age of networked knowledge.

As a result, millions of people are unhappy at work, organizations are operating well below their potential, leaders like you are frustrated, and almost everyone feels stressed out. In spite of the recent uptick in the economy, no one I know believes things are working the way they should be.

At one level the problem is simple: the world has changed, but the way we lead and engage people has not. There is a terrible misalignment between the work and the workforce, on the one hand, and our leadership models and practices, on the other.

As *Fast Company* founder Alan Webber pointed out over twenty years ago, conversation is at the very heart of knowledge-based work. Yet most of us don't recognize how dependent we are on conversations for learning, for making sense of our experiences, for building relationships, for innovation, and for sorting out how we feel about ourselves and our work.

My basic goal is to enhance organizational performance, but my passion is to improve the daily experiences of those millions of people who feel unhappy, disengaged, and under-utilized at work.

The beauty of the way knowledge-based organizations operate is that the more engaged—and the more respected—workers are, the more productive they are, and the happier their customers are as well. And almost all successful organizations today are knowledge-based; even retail stores and factories depend on people who are well-educated, computer-literate, and self-directed.

The best way to improve the work experience—and to enhance productivity, increase engagement, and make work fun again— is to change the way all those meetings are designed, led, and experienced.

You've heard all about low employee engagement and excessive employee turnover as organizations struggle to create attractive work environments and opportunities for satisfying work.

The best, most effective way of addressing those serious organizational challenges isn't by attacking them directly. It is by rethinking and transforming those millions of meetings and other corporate conversations that take place in hallways, offices, and conference rooms around the globe.

Too many of us don't know how to talk to—make that "talk *with*"—each other about things that matter. We don't know how to listen thoughtfully, and we don't know how to blend diverse insights, ideas, and experiences into coherent and creative solutions. Frankly, we aren't very good at encouraging others to engage with us in meaningful conversations.

Let me amend that: most of us already do know how to talk with each other. We do it all the time at home, at social gatherings, in pubs and coffee houses, and wherever we meet each other *outside* the workplace.

Curiously, however, we don't seem to have the right conversational mindset at work. We may have a conversational *skillset*, but we don't use it effectively to draw out the latent talent, ideas, and insights that are locked inside the heads of our fellow employees.

In my experience, most team and meeting leaders seem to believe their primary role is to tell their staff what to do.

But *telling* isn't leading. Yes, part of the role of a leader is to articulate a compelling vision of the future, and to guide the team towards that goal; but in a world that's swimming in information and filled with knowledgeable people, leadership is really about enabling collaboration and group decision making on a grand scale. That means engaging people in meaningful conversations. As my friend

David Isaacs likes to put it, collaboration is the art of blending a collection of individual intelligences into a *collective intelligence*.

We Need New Rules—and Cool Tools—for the Digital Age

A senior Japanese technology executive and I were speaking about the future of work. In typical American overstatement I blurted out "Technology is changing everything!" He responded immediately, "Then we have to change everything about the way we manage."

I think about that exchange often, because at the time I thought he was exaggerating (and of course I knew I was). But now, in hindsight, I don't think either one of us realized how insightful that conversation was.

As I have already suggested, the world has changed so much that we have to change the way we lead organizations, teams, and especially the conversations we engage in on a daily basis. In this book I propose a number of "rules" for generating engaging conversations and productive meetings.

Some of them, especially those that take digital technologies into account, are new, but many have been around for decades. I will also suggest several new—and very cool—tools that can make your conversations soar.

However, this is not a book about technology. I have no desire to see technology replacing thoughtful leadership or meaningful conversations. Yet in this world of networked knowledge, where we connect with others halfway around the world as easily and inexpensively as with our colleagues across the hallway, we have become highly dependent on technology to make those connections come alive. So it is important that we apply technology thoughtfully.

Like any other tools, collaborative technologies are only as helpful as we choose to make them.

Strength in Numbers

If there is one foundational principle I want you to embrace, it is this: *No one—no single individual—is smarter than everyone.*

I first heard that assertion from former business executive and author Rod Collins, and I will be forever grateful to him for that wonderful way of capturing such an important idea. We are far more capable as members of a cohesive team or a collective "hive mind" than we are as individuals. There is strength in numbers. It does take a village. We can accomplish so much more together than we can separately.

One more time: the way we work has changed, fundamentally and forever. Technology has transformed the way we access and publish information, as well as the way we communicate with each other and form relationships. But that's only the beginning: work itself has changed as well, and so have the people doing that work.

As Father John Culkin, SJ, of Fordham University, suggested many years ago in a conversation with Marshall McLuhan, "We shape our tools and then our tools shape us."

Except that, as I believe, habits built during the industrial revolution have become so ingrained that most organizational leaders don't seem to recognize how much the world has changed. They are failing to take advantage of the new tools that are reshaping how we communicate, how we work, and how we learn. Worse, their beliefs and attitudes are actively preventing their organizations from thriving in this new age of networked knowledge.

Father Culkin wasn't wrong; he just didn't realize how long it would take for these new tools to reshape us.

Don't let yourself be, or remain, an industrial-age leader. From this day forward embrace the new economy, take advantage of the new tools, and come with me on an exciting journey into the future of work.

We must learn all over again how to enable constructive conversations in this age of networked knowledge. But let's go way beyond merely *rethinking* those conversations. Until we *transform* the way we engage with each other at work we are doomed to continuing anger, frustration, and subpar organizational performance.

Your Leadership Opportunity—and Your Obligation

As an organizational leader you have an incredible opportunity—and an equally important responsibility. What you do and say on a daily basis affects the lives and the careers of everyone you come in contact with, to say nothing of the impact you have on your organization's performance and its ultimate success or failure in the marketplace.

Your opportunity—and your responsibility—is to create a social, technical, and physical environment that enables your staff to thrive, and to contribute their ideas, insights, and experiences to your organization. The best way I know to accomplish that noble end is to ensure that all your conversations at work are respectful, focused, candid, and collaborative. If you would like to watch a brief video commentary about the ideas in this book, please go to http://www.makingmeetingsmatter.com/overviewvideo.

Now, let's get to work.

Chapter 1

WHAT'S GOING ON?

Employee engagement is at an all-time low. According to a 2013 Gallup survey, more than 70 percent of the workforce is not engaged. In the average company about 20 percent of employees are *actively* disengaged, which Gallup defines as either wandering around in a fog avoiding all work responsibilities, or in some extreme cases deliberately undermining their co-workers' success.

As a result of the recession over the past several years, workers are more bummed out, burned out, and stressed out than ever. A survey by Right Management at the depth of the Great Recession found that 83 percent of the workforce intended to look for a new job when the economy improved and another 9 percent were networking to explore possibilities. That means you could be at risk of losing more than 90 percent of your workforce!

We are in the middle of a fundamental revolution in the way we live, work, communicate, collaborate, and learn, and the workforce is voting with its feet. The economic recovery is presenting capable workers with more options, and they are taking advantage of them.

What's going on? In this opening chapter I argue that the way we live and work has changed so dramatically in the last twenty years that our basic leadership beliefs and practices are no longer appropriate. We have information and tools at our disposal that were unheard of, and even unimaginable, just a few decades ago.

But the way we are trying to manage is still mired in nineteenth-century assumptions about people, technology, economic value, and social well-being. The dominant "Command-and-Control" mind-set of most executives is out of sync with the world as it now operates.

And that misalignment shows up most prominently in the millions of corporate meetings that take place every day. If you can learn to talk with your staff and colleagues more respectfully, more candidly, and with more curiosity, you will not only feel better about your work experiences, you will also learn more, be more creative, and generate more value for your customers and shareholders.

The Misalignment between Work and Leadership

There are at least four reasons for this misfit between the work and the workforce, on one hand, and the dominant style of "Command-and-Control" leadership, on the other:

- Technology has fundamentally changed the way we communicate, learn, and make sense of the world we live in.

- The nature of work itself has changed as we transition from an industrial economy to an information and knowledge-based one.

- Our social values and expectations have evolved. Today we value different kinds of things and experiences than we did forty or fifty years ago. Many of us today have ambitious goals for our lives, our friendships, and our global community—goals that seem increasingly difficult to attain.

■ Most leadership development and training programs
continue to teach "Command-and-Control" techniques;
we are not preparing leaders adequately for the new
conditions they face every day at work.

This new world makes most of us hungry for a new kind of work
experience, and for a new kind of organizational leader, because
so many of the leaders we know do not seem aligned with this
new reality. You want your experiences at work to be enriching,
remarkable, and memorable yet most of the time they are
anything but.

You want to work with and for people who don't just tell you what
to do but rather enable you to do what you do best. You want to
feel successful, valued, and respected for who you are. And you
want to make a difference.

The good news is that there are many living examples of
organizations that do work that way and that create fun,
engaging, and incredibly productive work environments. I want
to make sure you know about them, and that you understand not
only how they work, but why they are so successful.

The bad news is that organizations that are thriving in these
new conditions are still few and far between. Far too many
organizations and their leaders are still operating as if it's the 1950s.

The Way We Were

Some of us can still remember when our families sat down in
front of the big box in our living rooms that brought us the six
o'clock evening news. Here in the United States we shared that
experience with our neighbors near and far; most of the country
absorbed the news at the same time, and it all came from one of
the three major television networks.

Conditions were relatively similar in other countries. As I understand it, at one time in England there was the BBC and nothing else.

We also relied heavily on printed newspapers and magazines that were delivered to our front doors in the morning or evening, or with the daily mail. Time and Newsweek were the primary, and almost the only, source of national news.

Most households had one telephone somewhere in the front hall or living room; but it was only used for short, functional conversations with neighbors and nearby relatives (calls were billed by the minute, after all). Once a year we might call a distant grandparent for a short "Happy Birthday" or "Happy Holidays" message; long-distance calls were prohibitively expensive and the sound was often tinny and full of static.

In short, we didn't have much choice in how we got our information or stayed in touch with out-of-town family and friends. Our world was relatively limited.

And the way we worked was very similar.

Those of us who worked in an office typically commuted to a downtown business district or a suburban office park. Most people stayed with one company for many years (often an entire career). Both my father and my grandfather retired from the companies they joined right after they graduated from college; and both of those companies were large, stable, and relatively successful over many decades (although both have had serious ups and downs in the last decade).

That world of the twentieth century clearly reflected the values and assumptions of the industrial era; that the goal of an organization was mass production (accompanied, of course, by mass consumption). Drive costs down by driving volume up; produce as many widgets as possible at the lowest possible cost.

Everyone was focused on figuring out the most efficient way to produce and sell those products. Reliable, reproducible processes were the end goal.

Most social structures and community activities were just as stable. Many of today's senior executives grew up in the same town where they were born: their friendships began in kindergarten and lasted at least through secondary school. Neighborhoods were incredibly homogeneous, and expectations of career opportunities were shaped largely by the socioeconomic class and the community one was born into.

There was a strong sense of stability in that world. Yes, there was a sense of progress and a desire to climb the economic ladder, but most change was linear and incremental. Our sense of what was possible was almost as limited as our choice of television stations.

The leadership culture in too many organizations today still reflects that era: There are hidden assumptions that information is scarce, that the job of managers is to tell their subordinates what to do, and that power comes from being in control.

Technology Has Changed All That

Today, of course, all that has changed (or most of it, anyway). We now have access to incredibly powerful personal computing devices; most of us work in offices, not factories; and our basic social norms and values are profoundly different than they were five or ten or twenty years ago—to say nothing of six months ago.

There are at least three very profound ways that our information access and personal communications have changed in the last decade—three realities that most of the world takes for granted today, but that are absolutely unprecedented in human history.

First, with a relatively inexpensive computer and an Internet connection, **anyone can access almost any information almost**

anywhere in the world—and at almost no incremental cost. Granted, digital data is only part of the information that matters. Nevertheless, you can find almost anything you want whenever you want it, with very little advance planning, somewhere online. Just type your question or topic into your favorite search engine, and start digging.

Second, **you can connect and converse with almost any other person, almost anywhere in the world**, again at almost zero incremental cost. And you have an incredible array of ways to connect. Landline phones still work, and e-mail is essentially free and easy. Cell phones are everywhere (though they do have a basic fixed cost, the incremental minutes are relatively cheap). And don't forget all the other communication channels that are readily available, many of them completely free once you have online access: Skype, LinkedIn, Facebook, Twitter, Instagram, Snapchat, Tumblr, Flickr, Facetime, Pinterest, Periscope, Blab, and more.

And third, **anyone with a computer and an Internet connection can publish almost anything on a global basis**. While no one has an accurate count of how many blogs there are globally, the three major blogging platforms (Tumblr, Wordpress, and Blogger) together had over 300 million accounts at the end of 2014.

And then of course there is YouTube and other video platforms. YouTube's video library grows by one hundred hours *every single minute of every single day*—that's over 144,000 hours of new video per day! And over 6 *billion* hours of video are viewed every day (that's almost an hour per day for every person on earth). Yes, viewing recorded video isn't exactly a real conversation, but it certainly is an increasingly popular means of communicating ideas.

It is all too common to hear people lamenting that all this social media is replacing in-person conversation, and that young people especially seem to have lost the art of conversing. While there may be some legitimate cause for concern, coffee houses and neighborhood bars are more popular than ever. There appears to be plenty of animated conversation within our society; it just doesn't seem to happen in the workplace very often.

So far I haven't even mentioned the 500-plus channels of cable television that are available here in the United States alone, and most of that video content is now available on the Internet as well.

Admittedly, much of what is published or uploaded isn't the least bit interesting to many of us. But it's there to be read or viewed or listened to. This explosive growth in the amount of information and communication being sent out and received is nothing short of staggering. There is no question we're having an unprecedented global conversation; but most of these global "conversations" (using the term in its broadest form) take place *outside* the workplace.

Work Itself Has Also Changed

The basic experiences we have at work today are also very different from the past and we produce value in ways that were unimaginable just a few years ago.

Early in my career I worked for a large mid-western textbook publishing firm. I have never forgotten a conversation with one editor, a brilliant, well-educated woman, who told me in tears that she had just been docked a full week's vacation.

My friend was supposed to be at her desk and at work every morning at 8:30 a.m.; her supervisor had been tracking her arrivals and had documented that over the past twelve months she had accumulated almost forty hours of tardiness (ten minutes one day, five minutes another, and so on). It apparently made no difference that she almost never joined the parade out the door at precisely 5 p.m.; in fact she regularly worked an hour or two beyond 5 p.m. to meet her deadlines. And she often took work home at night.

Docking her vacation time might have been an appropriate disciplinary action if my friend had been working on an assembly line somewhere and was being paid by the hour. But she was a former secondary school teacher with a master's degree who was being paid a decent salary to collaborate with a college professor on a high-school math book.

Knowledge workers are different, and they work differently from assembly line workers. If you think about it, that's obvious. But in my experience an incredible number of supposedly intelligent organizational leaders don't seem to understand how different knowledge-based work is.

Knowledge is not a "thing" that you can hold in your hand, or even describe. It doesn't have weight, or color, or smell. There are all kinds of knowledge. There is information, or data, and "facts" about the physical world. There is an understanding of how physical objects behave, or interact with each other; how one thing can cause another, or how one chemical interacts with another (for example, how detergent neutralizes acidic juices).

There is also knowledge about patterns in nature, or in human relationships. The sun rises and sets on a predictable cycle; summer follows spring; water freezes at thirty-two degrees Fahrenheit. Some so-called "knowledge" is more tenuous; and when it is based on opinions or beliefs that do not have any basis in reality it can be downright dangerous.

But what makes knowledge really different from physical things is what you can do with it (and what you can't). For example, if I have one hundred dollars and give you half of it, now you have fifty dollars and I have fifty dollars. But if I have a special recipe for roasting a chicken and I share it with you, now we both know how to cook a delicious meal. I haven't given up anything, but now there are two of us who have the same knowledge (in fact, I probably gained some credibility and gratitude for sharing my special recipe so willingly). Furthermore, once information has been shared it can't be taken back. Once I've told you that recipe I can't "untell" you.

Our economy's growing dependence on information and knowledge as the source of value has profound implications for how we form teams, collaborate, and manage both work and workers.

We bring our individual experiences, expectations, and learning and communication styles to the work we do; work is now an expression of who we are and what we care about.

It's no longer about putting in eight hours on the assembly line and doing the exact same things your peers are doing (over and over and over again).

In the industrial era most organizations were seeking workers who had mastered a common core of skills and who were capable of "tending" the machines on the assembly line; workers were essentially replaceable because each station on that assembly line required the same skills and the same behaviors no matter who the individual worker was.

But when a knowledge worker joins a team the very nature of the team changes—its capabilities, its collective mindset, even its norms and expectations. Each of us is a unique individual who brings a unique combination of experiences, knowledge, and skills to work.

But there's even more to this social and economic transformation we are experiencing. Along with all the new technology and the transformation of work itself we are also undergoing a dramatic shift in social values and expectations.

New Social Values and Expectations

The best way I can describe how social values and expectations are changing is with a personal story. When my son, who is now an accomplished web designer, was in his late teens he informed his mother and me that he didn't want any job where he had to wear a tie. As he put it, "I don't want to work fifty weeks a year so I can take a two-week vacation doing what I really care about." In his mind, "work" meant being a wage slave at some large corporation doing what you were told to do and he was having none of it.

Today my son CJ works forty to fifty hours a week (for himself), but he does it on his own terms. He lives in the mountains. During the winter he often takes two or three hours in the morning to ski, and then stays at his desk until 7 or 8 p.m. In good weather he takes a spin on his mountain bike almost every day, and he's bought a small sailboat that he loves to get out on the water at sunset during the summer. He's living a wonderfully balanced life, earning a decent living, and happier by far than many more affluent technology entrepreneurs who are putting in seventy- or eighty-hour work weeks.

CJ's experience and his values remind me of a classic parable that's well worth repeating in its entirety. I found this version (there are many variations) on the website www.financialmentor.com (which interestingly enough is focused on helping clients retire successfully).

Here's the parable of the Mexican Fisherman and the Investment Banker:

> An American investment banker was taking a much-needed vacation in a small coastal Mexican village when a small boat with just one fisherman docked. The boat had several large, fresh fish in it.

The investment banker was impressed by the quality of the fish and asked the Mexican how long it took to catch them.

The Mexican replied, "Only a little while."

The banker then asked why he didn't stay out longer and catch more fish?

The Mexican fisherman replied he had enough to support his family's immediate needs.

The American then asked "But what do you do with the rest of your time?"

The Mexican fisherman replied, "I sleep late, fish a little, play with my children, take siesta with my wife, stroll into the village each evening where I sip wine and play guitar with my amigos: I have a full and busy life, señor."

The investment banker scoffed, "I am an Ivy League MBA, and I could help you. You could spend more time fishing and with the proceeds buy a bigger boat, and with the proceeds from the bigger boat you could buy several boats until eventually you would have a whole fleet of fishing boats. Instead of selling your catch to the middleman you could sell directly to the processor, eventually opening your own cannery. You could control the product, processing, and distribution."

Then he added, "Of course, you would need to leave this small coastal fishing village and move to Mexico City where you would run your growing enterprise."

The Mexican fisherman asked, "But señor, how long will this all take?"

To which the American replied, "Fifteen to twenty years."

"But what then?" asked the Mexican.

The American laughed and said, "That's the best part. When the time is right you would announce an IPO and sell your company stock to the public and become very rich. You could make millions."

"Millions, señor? Then what?"

To which the investment banker replied, "Then you would retire. You could move to a small coastal fishing village where you would sleep late, fish a little, play with your kids, take siesta with your wife, and stroll to the village in the evenings where you could sip wine and play your guitar with your amigos."

I don't think you need me to tell you the point of that story.

The Changing Cultural Landscape

While my son and the Mexican fisherman may not be fully representative of today's cultural norms and expectations, their mindsets exemplify something that many of us feel: there is something missing, and out of order, with the world that evolved out of the industrial-age emphasis on large organizations and climbing the corporate ladder as the ultimate evidence of success.

There is a growing level of disaffection and frustration with the work experience today. Just look at the titles of some of the most recent popular business books:

- *Why Work Sucks*, by Cali Ressler and Jody Thompson

- *The Shift*, by Lynda Gratton

- *Management Shift*, by Vladke Huptic

- *The Work Revolution*, by Julie Clow

- *Rebooting Work*, by Maynard Webb
- *Mavericks at Work*, by William C. Taylor and Polly Labore
- *The Fifth Age of Work,* by Andrew Jones
- *Coming Alive: The Journey to Reengage Your Life and Your Career*, by Ruth Ross

(You can find more information about each of these books, in the Resources and Notes section at the end of the book)

There are also many formal and informal organizations and virtual communities that are dedicated to transforming the workplace so it more accurately and more appropriately reflects the new social values.

For example, Josh Allan Dykstra and several colleagues have formed a virtual community called **The Work Revolution** (www.workrevolution.org) that describes itself as a "movement and advocacy group that promotes human and meaningful work for everyone."

There are also several centers of influence on college and university campuses that are seeking to transform the way organizations are governed and led, and the way future organizational leaders learn about how to create value.

Take a look, for example, at the Center for Positive Organizations at the Ross School of Business at the University of Michigan (http://positiveorgs.bus.umich.edu/). That center's mission is: "to inspire and enable leaders to build high-performing organizations that bring out the best in people. We are a catalyst for the creation and growth of positive organizations."

And I have personally been involved in launching **The Great Work Cultures** community (www.greatworkcultures.org), a group that seeks to connect the multitude of disparate and diverse groups like the Work Revolution, and to create a "big tent" that connects and promotes many of the individual groups that are calling for new ways of working.

Great Work Cultures has a simple but profound credo:

> Great Work Cultures is dedicated to unleashing the power within human organizations. We hold that the primary purpose of an organization is to create value for all the people it serves.
>
> We believe in:
>
> • Collaboration over control
>
> • Human Experience over bureaucratic rules
>
> • Networks over hierarchies
>
> While the items on the right have value, we value the items on the left more.

Those ideas have had a major influence on my own thinking, and have helped me find a voice for expressing the insights and beliefs I have developed from over thirty years at work in the corporate world.

There is lots of attention being paid these days to generational differences, and to Millennials as representatives of a vague but vastly transformed future. Some observers and pundits find that future exciting and encouraging, while others find it depressing.

No matter what you think about that future, by 2020 close to half of the workforce will be what we currently call "Millennials"— people born between about 1982 and 2004 (that definition comes from researchers Neil Howe and William Straus, the authors of another important book on the future of work titled *The Fourth Turning*—see Resources and Notes for more information).

Certainly there are massive differences between the work and personal experiences that younger workers have had growing up, and the experiences that those of us "of a certain age" with gray hair, or no hair, can recall. However, when the Millennials dominate the workforce in 2020 they will range in age from about twenty to thirty-eight years old.

It's safe to assume that most of the older Millennials will be married, raising children, and just as preoccupied with many of the same kinds of parenting, social, and environmental issues that we older folks fret about today.

But no matter how old you are, you are painfully aware of issues and challenges in other parts of the world. Although there are obvious ethnic and regional differences, jet airplanes, television, and the Internet have combined to create a truly global village.

Technology has connected us with each other and with other "neighborhoods" in the global village in ways that we are still struggling to understand.

On the one hand, we often seem to depend more on e-mail and text messages today than on real-time personal conversations, whether they are face-to-face or by telephone (or Skype, or any of the many other online collaborative technologies that we now use on a daily basis).

On the other hand, we are more aware of natural disasters and other events both tragic and celebratory no matter where in the world they occur. And the workforce of today and tomorrow has grown up during a time of immense and sometimes violent political conflict all over the world (including right here in the United States). I believe this awareness of the fragility of life has driven many people back to basics; family, friends, nature, art, and recreation have become increasingly important to the quality of life.

Of course, our relative affluence and general good health (in spite of the twin epidemics of obesity and diabetes) have also enabled us to pay more attention to the higher-order aspects of life like self-esteem and self-actualization.

It seems clear that our general awareness of the injustices and suffering in other parts of the world, along with other global challenges, directly impacts our attitudes toward authority figures and our expectations about how we want to be treated in the workplace.

Moreover, the boundaries between the workplace and that bigger world are far more porous than they have ever been. It's now incredibly easy to sit in your office at work and exchange e-mails or phone calls with family members, caretakers, medical care professionals, investment advisors, and your car mechanic. You can order books, DVDs, home furniture, food, and clothing online, or pay your bills, during your lunch hour.

Of course you can also read and respond to your work e-mails from your living room, the airport, the train station, or in bed just before you turn out the light. The workplace isn't an isolated, insulated environment any more and your employees are part of a wide network of relationships and commitments that affect the work they do every day—just as their work affects their personal lives.

Why is this important? Because our experiences outside of work have a far more direct impact on how we work and how we relate to our colleagues today than they ever did in the industrial era. It used to be that punching the time clock at the start of the work day meant turning off your personality and your individuality.

Now, it's just the opposite. Your employer and your work colleagues depend on you to express yourself on the job. That's what knowledge work is all about: sharing ideas, being creative, and applying your unique knowledge to the task at hand.

People now come into work expecting to be part of a community, to be listened to, and to be respected and recognized for what they know and what they do. After all, that's what they experience with their family and friends; why should it be any different at work?

Rethinking Leadership

For at least the last 150 years (and actually well before that) leadership has meant being in charge. Leaders took command and exercised control because they knew more than their subordinates, or they had more power. Originally, of course, power meant physical strength, or control over powerful resources, like armies or ships, and weapons.

For over a century most organizational leaders have embraced the concept of "Scientific Management" generally credited to Frederick Taylor, who first applied time-and-motion analysis to work in the early 1900s. Taylor argued that the job of managers was to *think*, and the job of workers was to do. Anyone who challenged a manager's directions was viewed as insubordinate.

It is becoming very clear that the management practices that worked very well in an era of mass production are essentially inappropriate for this new era of mass collaboration—an economy in which economic value and competitive advantage come from collaborative innovation, creativity, and working with customers to address and solve problems, not from low-cost commodities.

We know intuitively that organizational direction isn't established or implemented by single individuals, but the media and the dominant business schools continue to foster the myth of leadership as a direction-setting and deciding activity engaged in by a very few highly capable individuals.

That may have been somewhat true during the industrial era. But it's patently false and dangerously misleading in the twenty-first century. As author and former business executive Rod Collins likes to point out, power today comes from being connected, not from being "in control."

My friend David Isaacs told me recently that, in his twenty-plus years of showing organizations how to achieve higher levels of consciousness and effectiveness, every organization he has worked with has already had within it all the knowledge and talent it needed to succeed. Unfortunately, however, many organizational leaders don't know how to tap into the diverse experiences, knowledge, and skills that are abundant all around them.

Today anyone charged with leading knowledge workers or accomplishing a knowledge-generation task must come to grips with a new role: enabling sense-making and problem-solving through collaboration. The skills that are critical for team leaders today are those related to encouraging dialogue and debate, fostering open and candid conversation, and guiding or coaching (not controlling) their staff towards high-quality solutions.

I am convinced that the Command-and-Control culture, which remains prevalent in so many organizations today, is the primary reason we have such low levels of employee engagement and such high levels of employee turnover (even in the soft economy we're still fighting to get out of).

Furthermore, that Command-and-Control mindset drives most of those frustrating meetings you experience almost every day. Too many leaders still see their job as directing the activities of their subordinates, not as drawing out (and benefiting from) the incredible diversity of skills, experiences, and ideas that those people have to offer.

Think about this for a moment: when you were in college did your professor ever tell you where to read the homework assignment or what time to write the term paper? No, of course not. There were classes you could choose to attend, and there was a required exam, but other than that, you were treated as a responsible adult fully capable of making your own choices about where, when, and how to study.

Some of us took advantage of that freedom and blew off some of our classes or even entire courses. But most of us learned how to make the choices that gave us both a good time and a good education.

So what happens when newly-hired recruits walk into a corporation? They're told in so many words, "Be in that seat at 8:30 a.m. and stay there until 5:30 p.m. — and in the meantime, be creative." That is almost exactly what was said to my former business partner Charlie Grantham on the day he started work at a very large, well-known telecommunications company.

Tragically, however, most formal leadership training and development programs still operate from a perspective that defines a leader as the person "in charge." Corporate leaders are still seen as all-powerful and in command. The popular business magazines continue to feature stories of CEOs and other senior executives depicting them as wise, visionary, benevolent individuals who sit above the fray and look out into the future, sharing their magical insights with the masses.

But Command-and-Control is the wrong way to manage creative talent or produce innovative outcomes. We need to reinvent leadership as an activity that blends and leverages the capabilities that every single individual brings to the workplace every single day.

Looking Ahead

That's my sense of what's going on today and what's wrong with the way most organizations are being led and managed. But while I've hinted at my vision of what's possible, I haven't spelled it out in any detail. In Chapter 2 we'll look at several examples of how effective knowledge-based organizations operate. These stories will help you understand what's possible when an organization's leaders discover the power of tapping into the talent that is so abundant in every organization. I am convinced that when you change your mindset about the meetings and other conversations that take place every day in your organization you will transform the culture, and that in turn will transform your business outcomes.

Chapter Two

WELL-DESIGNED MEETINGS CAN MAKE A DIFFERENCE

I wrote this book because I believe there are huge rewards for getting beyond Command and Control leadership. Your meetings—and conversations of all kinds—will matter when you adopt a mindset filled with curiosity, respect for others, and a genuine desire to solve problems, produce value for your customers, and enjoy the conversations you engage in every day at work.

Furthermore, I believe the best way to increase engagement, make work fun, and enhance organizational performance is to attack the problem at its roots. We spend more time in corporate meetings than in just about any other activity. So if we first understand why there are so many bad meetings and then look at what some organizations are doing to make their meetings both productive and fun, we can begin finding our way out of this dark forest we've wandered into.

Why Are There So Many Bad Meetings?

There don't seem to be any definitive statistics about how many meetings are held every day, but the estimates I have seen (and recalculated for myself) suggest that there are somewhere between eleven and twenty-four million corporate meetings a day in the United States alone. Even though that is a wide range, I am confident that there at least *four billion meetings a year!* However, as I am fond of saying, no one I know is dying for that next meeting to start.

Yet most people who work in offices today spend most of their time in meetings of one kind or another. Some studies claim that project team leaders and department managers typically spend between 40 percent and 60 percent of their work week in meetings of one kind or another. That amounts to well over twenty hours a week, not counting the time they spend preparing for those meetings or writing up post-meeting reports.

As Alan Webber, former editor of the *Harvard Business Review* and co-founder of *Fast Company*, observed over twenty years ago, conversation is at the heart of knowledge-based work. It's how we exchange information, solve problems, test our ideas, create new knowledge, and connect with our colleagues and customers.

If we spend so many working hours in meetings of one kind or another, why do so many of them turn out so badly? I believe there are at least five factors affecting the quality of your meeting experiences:

- **We are already swimming in a sea of information.** Meetings have served traditionally as an efficient means of sharing consistent information with a group of people who *need to know*. A team leader calls everyone into a conference room to report news to the group or to ask the participants to share project updates.

  Yet digital technology today provides most of that kind of information more quickly and more accurately, and in formats that can be fine-tuned to individual needs. Whether it's e-mail, Twitter, Jabber, Yammer, instant messaging, or project status websites, everyone who needs to know what's going on can get updates while sitting at their workstations, or on mobile devices no matter where they are physically.

Stopping everything else to sit in a closed conference room for an hour or more just doesn't make the same kind of sense it used to.

- **It's too easy to call meetings—and there is little accountability for results.** It's just too easy for a team or department leader to schedule a meeting. Hardly anyone publishes a formal agenda or a statement of desired outcomes in advance of a meeting.

   And I can't recall ever hearing a meeting leader identify the full corporate cost of a meeting—not just the meeting room and refreshments, but the combined salary cost of all the participants. Rick Gilbert, author of *Speaking Up: Surviving Executive Presentations*, estimates that a one-hour meeting of C-Suite executives can cost more than $35,000! Too often a meeting is simply the default approach no matter what the need is.

- **Many meeting leaders don't define or explain their purpose or the desired process clearly.** There are many different reasons for calling a meeting; and the appropriate conversation process varies dramatically depending on the meeting's purpose and desired outcomes. An informational meeting should unfold differently from a decision-making meeting, which in turn is different from a creative brainstorming meeting. Yet all too often participants arrive at the meeting without any understanding of the agenda, the intended process, or the desired outcomes.

- **Most organizational cultures discourage candid conversation.** When meetings are fun, respectful, and engaging the participants are curious, exploring ideas, listening actively, learning new and meaningful ideas, and often constructively challenging each other. But in many organizations today the dominant behavioral norms discourage even mild disagreements.

One of the biggest enemies of meaningful meetings is the tendency towards groupthink and an unwillingness to engage in any active discourse. Challenging someone's idea, or offering alternative approaches, means taking responsibility for conflict and change, and that can be stressful.

- **Many of us are not effective listeners and learners.** The high levels of stress and overwork that affect so many of us these days make it genuinely difficult to hear ideas or arguments that run counter to our own experience and preferences. New ideas, or ideas that might complicate our own work, are hard to absorb. So we tend to shut them out, or at least dismiss them as not important or not doable.

NEW RULE: Mindsets are more important than skillsets

But this is not another book about how to run a meeting. There are hundreds, if not thousands, of good books full of tips, tactics, and techniques for planning meetings, for orchestrating meaningful conversations, and for moving from conversations to commitments. In fact, I have listed several of my favorite how-to-run-meetings books in Resources and Notes at the end of the book.

Most of us with any organizational experience at all know in our guts what a good meeting looks and feels like. Yet we don't practice what we preach (and we too often don't demand it of our leaders either); most corporate meetings continue to be unproductive, unimaginative, and incredibly frustrating for everyone.

What's going on?

My view, and the reason I wrote this book, is that most of us who lead meetings misunderstand what they are good for. We think of meetings as a way to tell people what to do, or to persuade them to get something done. We don't think of meetings as a way to draw out the insights, ideas, and experiences of a diverse, multi-talented group of people—or to meld a diverse group into a cohesive team. We don't recognize the value of blending individual talents into a collective intelligence.

In short, we approach meetings with the wrong mindset.

If we change our mindsets, we'll change our conversations. And if we change our conversations we will change our cultures, and ultimately our individual and team performance.

Stanford Professor Carol Dweck tells a marvelous story about a Chicago-area high school I wish I'd attended. When students receive a report card on a course they have not passed, the grade they get is "Not Yet." Not "Failed," but rather *"Not Yet."*

Think about that for a moment. For Professor Dweck, and for me, that choice of wording is incredibly powerful.

What does "Not Yet" say to that student? It does not say, "You are stupid, you are a loser, you can't do it." Instead it says "You didn't pass *this time.*" It presumes there will be another time, and it also tells the student "You might pass the course the next time you try."

Professor Dweck has been studying achievement, learning, and happiness for a long time. She's written a book called *Mindset* (Ballantine Books, 2007) in which she identifies two very different ways of experiencing life. And while most of her research has focused on young children and adolescents, her insights are equally important for adults in the workplace.

She describes two distinctively different attitudes, or mindsets, about success and failure (or rather, success and "Not Yet"). Many children develop what Dweck calls a *fixed* mindset—one that presumes a person's intelligence, physical skills, and personality are fixed. That mindset believes that we are who we are, that we can't, and don't change, with new experiences.

In contrast, children who develop a *growth* mindset, believe they can learn, improve their skills, and even change their personalities over time. People with a growth mindset view difficult problems as learning opportunities. They relish challenges, and they thrive on learning new ideas and new skills.

As I've been reviewing my own experiences and working on this book, I have become convinced that the process of leading meetings that matter and designing effective conversations in the workplace is far less about having the right skills and much more about having a growth mindset.

Leaders who relish learning and want to develop their staff's knowledge and skills conduct meetings that are open, interactive, and collaborative. They want to learn from others' experiences, and to hear how their colleagues think about a particular problem, challenge, or business opportunity. They believe deep down that a team can do more than a collection of individuals—that the "wisdom of the crowd" is real and that we are smarter together.

Effective leaders aren't threatened by other people who see the world differently, or have different backgrounds and educations; effective leaders thrive on drawing those experiences and ideas out of their staff to create new products, new marketing campaigns, new ways of reporting financial performance.

However, it is far easier for me to say "You need a new mindset" than it is for you to just put one on like a new hat or sweater. As

Dweck's research clearly shows, new mindsets grow out of new experiences.

Thus, my goal is to persuade you to try planning and leading your meetings and other conversations differently, see what happens, and learn by doing. As some wise person observed many years ago, it is usually easier to act your way into a new kind of thinking than it is to think yourself into a new way of acting.

I intend to show you that leading meetings differently (and preparing for them differently) does in fact change the quality of everyone's experience. That's the goal of this chapter: to show you, through a variety of stories and examples, that meetings can not only be fun, they can also be FUNctional (pun intended)— engaging, productive, and even popular. You can make your meetings matter.

Running through the stories below is an important theme: when corporate conversations start feeling like personal conversations among friends, they become meaningful and engaging again.

I will show you just how much fun meetings can be when they are planned and led as natural, informal (but purposeful) gatherings of people who:

- Like and respect each other; and

- Share a common purpose or goal.

NEW RULE: Data builds understanding; stories build commitment

According to Alice Dee, a director of workplace services at Odyssey Enterprises, a large North American retailer (the name is disguised), meetings in that organization are filled with storytelling, and the presentations are heavily image-based, with very few words on very few individual presentation slides.

Instead of boring bullet points and slides filled to overflowing with data, Odyssey presentations feel more like personal stories, with heroes and villains, crises and victories, and lots of emotional content. Presenters influence and inspire through images, stories, and feelings rather than through hard data.

Even more intriguing, Dee told me that Odyssey meetings are incredibly non-traditional in other ways too. Most of the meeting rooms include a variety of brightly-colored lounge chairs, and participants are often standing on balance boards, sitting on exercise balls, or lying on the floor stretching their backs. It's how Odyssey employees take care of their physical as well as their mental wellbeing; and that informal, almost-anything-goes tone contributes richly to creativity, innovation, and a sense of anything is possible.

Dee mentioned that there are very few Odyssey meeting spaces with formal conference tables; most rooms have lounge furniture, informal wall coverings, unusual art objects. She also mentioned that many meetings at Odyssey are spontaneous; as a workplace services manager she is particularly pleased that the company has provided many different collaborative spaces so short-notice meetings are easy to hold.

In her words:

> In my experience the best ideas come from what I call "accidental collaboration." A couple of people see each other, start talking, perhaps move to a nearby unused space with a white board, and all of a sudden they've created a new product idea, or a new ad campaign. Having those places available without needing a reservation is what sparks new ideas over and over and over again.

Dee believes the culture at Odyssey is much stronger than at any other company she's worked with. The company has always valued inspiring stories of its customers' accomplishments, and Odyssey employees are constantly exposed to images that trigger emotional commitments rather than having to remember that third bullet point on the seventeenth slide.

Her description of how meetings unfold at Odyssey reminded me of my early experiences as a technology management consultant. Our firm often operated like the mythical character Johnny Appleseed, who collected and then shared all kinds of plant seeds as he traveled from one place to another along the American frontier.

Our consulting work often included client meetings that served as educational experiences, planting seeds of understanding about what was possible by sharing stories from other organizations. Our clients were not persuaded by data-based arguments about how productive some particular new technology was; they wanted to hear how other companies had used it and how it had affected both the bottom line and the day-to-day experiences of employees and customers.

The lesson from Odyssey's storytelling and informal meeting culture is clear:

The more natural a meeting is, in terms of atmosphere, meeting room layout, tone, connection to brand, and storytelling, the more likely it will produce innovative, meaningful ideas, insights, decisions, and commitments to action.

NEW RULE: Treat employees like human beings

Sue Bingham, the founder and principal of HPWP Consulting (High Performance Work Place Consulting), recalls with fondness the Monday morning staff meetings she led when she was a Corporate Training Manager for a large medical equipment supply company. As she told me, "my staff just loved those Monday morning meetings!"

Yes, you heard that right. Bingham and her seventeen-person staff couldn't wait for those weekly meetings to begin. How could that be?

Bingham described the way those meetings worked. each week two different staff members were responsible for supplying the group with breakfast—or at least some kind of decent food. Some people brought in store-bought donuts and other pastries. But once in a while someone would share home-made biscuits or scones. And one pair of enterprising would-be chefs actually brought a waffle iron to the office and cooked everyone hot waffles with butter and maple syrup.

But it wasn't just that little bit of humanity that personalized those meetings. At one point Bingham opened the meeting by asking what interesting things people had done over the weekend—kids' baseball games, hikes, picnics, etc. One Monday a couple of people mentioned movies they had seen and enjoyed over the weekend; someone else asked for a more extensive overview of one of the films, and before you knew it Monday mornings became movie review time.

Bingham learned to keep those movie reviews to no more than ten minutes each week, and was still able to cover all seventeen staff members' plans for the week in under an hour.

Those reviews became a Monday morning ritual the group eagerly looked forward to. In short, Bingham's team enjoyed each other's company, and looked forward to engaging conversations on Monday mornings as a way to reconnect with each other as well as to mark the inevitable transition back into the world of work that consumed them from Monday to Friday.

NEW RULE: Good ideas can come from anyone

Bill Sanders, a senior consultant with Roebling Straus, recalls an emergency meeting he participated in as a junior employee at one of his first jobs:

> I was working for a well-known consumer products company. We had just sold a large building in the Midwest that housed our largest data and call center. We had thirty days to vacate the building; senior management had just realized that we had to move the entire data center (without disrupting operations) in less than a month.
>
> Needless to say, panic set in.
>
> Although I was a very junior employee I was included in the crisis meeting. Many of us were in a conference room together; the CEO and several other senior executives were on the conference speaker phone.
>
> Most of the early comments were about the virtual impossibility of getting the entire data center moved and set up somewhere else on such short notice. The group seemed resigned to a horrible outcome.

As Sanders remembers, at one point he asked a simple question: "Who is buying the building?" Then he pointed out that the new owner only needed the space for their call center and wouldn't be setting up a data center anywhere near the size of the one his company had within the building. Then he asked, "Why don't we lease back part of the building and put a wall up to isolate our data center from theirs?"

That basic redefinition of the problem (from how to move the data center in less than thirty days to how to buy more time in order to move the data center in a rational, non-emergency way) changed everything.

Sanders wasn't bragging to me about his own brilliance; he gives full credit to the meeting leader (and the company CEO as well) for including and then listening to a very junior, inexperienced project manager and being willing to shift their whole mindset.

NEW RULE: Don't hold a meeting if you don't need one

Many people I know admit (privately) to being so bored with many meetings they are expected to attend to that they often invent excuses or schedule themselves to be somewhere else when a meeting they dread participating in shows up on their calendar.

The first rule for any leader to follow is to ask, "Is this meeting necessary?" I will deal more directly with how to answer that question in Chapter 3. For now, however, consider how Google once solved a critical system design problem without calling a single meeting (or even sending out a formal memo).

Eric Schmidt and Jonathan Rosenberg, in their highly compelling book *How Google Works*, tell the story of how in 2002 Google co-founder Larry Page was so disgusted with the output of the Google AdWords application that one Friday afternoon he printed out several examples of AdWords search results, stuck the printouts up on a bulletin board, scribbled "THESE ADS SUCK" in big letters across the printout, and stormed out of the office.

On Monday morning when Page and other Google staffers came in to begin the work week they found a 5 a.m. e-mail from one of the search engineers, Jeff Dean. Dean and a few colleagues had seen Page's note on the bulletin board on Friday afternoon. They completely agreed with his assessment.

But the Monday morning e-mail didn't just express their concurrence; it also contained a detailed analysis of why the search results were so bad, suggested a possible solution, included a live link to a prototype implementation of that solution that five of them had coded over the weekend, and offered some new search results as proof that their solution was worth considering.

That implementation, while crude and needing additional polishing, became the core of a complete transformation in the way AdWords worked—and created a new multibillion-dollar business for Google. What makes that particularly remarkable is that Dean and the other solution contributors were not even part of the AdWords design team; they were not personally responsible for the problem. However, they understood how important the ad searches were to Google, so they just did what they could to help.

What's the lesson? You don't need to call a meeting to define an obvious problem. And it's highly likely you wouldn't even invite the right people to that meeting. Don't hide the issue, or study it to death: broadcast it widely and let the skills you need come to you.

NEW RULE: Make the agenda the centerpiece of the meeting

When a meeting is the right thing to do, an agenda is not just a plan or a wish list or a way to tell people what the meeting is intended to be about. When used right, the agenda is the most critical tool you have to ensure that a meeting is worthwhile, covers the right topics, and accomplishes its purpose.

For example, Mark Parcell, a Senior Program Manager at a Salt Lake City high-tech company, uses the agenda for his weekly one-hour design review meetings as a primary planning tool as well as a means of enabling twenty-plus software engineers to make quick decisions on a number of critical design issues.

Parcell keeps a living agenda active in a Google docs file accessible to the meeting attendees at all times; he updates it regularly in advance of each week's meeting, so that if someone has no interest in or knowledge of any of the agenda items he or she can skip that week's meeting. Furthermore, the public agenda serves as notice that each issue scheduled to be addressed during that week's meeting will in fact be dealt with—everyone who does have a stake in that issue knows they need to attend the meeting.

As each weekly meeting begins Parcell projects the agenda on a screen in the conference room. He then works his way relentlessly through the agenda items.

As he told me,

> I'm painfully aware of how expensive these meetings are; everyone's time is valuable, and with twenty or more very smart engineers in that room I don't want to waste anyone's time. These design review meetings typically last fifty to sixty minutes and we'll cover thirty-five or more topics, so we have to move quickly. In most cases we are making decisions that affect many, many end users. We have to get it right, and we can't afford to avoid the issues either.

Parcell believes these meetings are effective, and popular, largely because there is a great deal of trust among the participants—in each other, in him, and in their responsibilities. Everyone knows how critical the decisions are; and they expect not only that everyone's voice will be heard but that the decisions will be made effectively and with the company's customers clearly in mind.

These design review meetings are characterized by intense debate. All the participants pay careful attention; many of them take notes on their laptops as the meeting unfolds; and those notes are also kept in a public online document that everyone in the meeting can access and read as they are being created (and afterwards as well). Thus not only is the original Agenda a public document, but so are the collaboratively-produced meeting Minutes.

Most of these meetings are over-packed with issues to be resolved, so they move along at a rapid pace. But if everything on the agenda is done early, Parcell cuts the meeting short; he doesn't feel any need to stretch it out. As he put it, "I'll say, 'We're done. You've got ten minutes to go get a breath of fresh air or just enjoy a few minutes of peace and quiet.' I don't want to waste anyone's time."

Parcell has also been known to cancel a meeting before it starts if the agenda feels thin or doesn't contain anything really urgent. Again, he knows how precious time is for his staff, and he's more than happy to give them a gift of a full sixty minutes of free time whenever he can.

NEW RULE: Don't let a fixed agenda prevent a good conversation

Benay Dara-Abrams has a different view of how agendas affect the quality of meetings. Like Mark Parcell, Dara-Abrams spent many years in Silicon Valley managing software design teams. But in her experience, sticking to an agenda too closely can produce a boring, meaningless meeting.

When I asked her what makes for a good conversation, she focused on the quality of the relationships among the participants, and emphasized the value of a free-flowing exchange of ideas that isn't bounded by arbitrary time constraints or a predetermined sequence of topics that has to be covered.

Dara-Abrams describes a good meeting this way:

> It starts with a shared purpose—a shared understanding of what the meeting is for, and what it's about. There is a genuine openness to what has to be discussed, and a sense

of good will—that everyone respects everyone else and is open to listening and learning.

The most important thing is to have a real conversation—a free flow of ideas and information. People should really feel free and open, not just reporting things or feeling like they have to watch what they are saying, or getting into groupthink—that tendency to say only what they think the meeting leader wants them to say.

I don't want to take a formal agenda too seriously; it can force the leader or facilitator to shut down an important conversation in order to keep to the pre-ordained time slots for each topic. I worry that being fixated on the agenda instead of the quality of the conversation can end up cutting off good ideas.

An agenda serves several important purposes; it communicates a meeting's objectives clearly in advance and it provides both the leader and the participants with a road map of the expected journey. However, as Dara-Abrams points out, adhering too closely to an advance agenda can cut short or derail meaningful conversations.

Time Out: Don't Those Two Rules Directly Contradict Each Other?

I just told two stories: Mark Parcell makes his agenda—and sticking to it—the centerpiece of his meetings. Benay Dara-Abrams, working in the same industry, argues that agendas get in the way of good conversations. How can they both be right?

Here's my take: this is a perfect example of the reality that there is no one set of rules that will make every meeting a great meeting.

Parcell's meetings are focused on resolving design inconsistencies. They bring a large group of busy software engineers together for a very dense hour of decision-making. Those meetings are not intended to generate great conversations; they are designed to produce a large number of important decisions in a very short time.

I suspect Dara-Abrams would be very comfortable adopting Parcell's directive style of leadership if she were leading that kind of meeting. Remember that I asked Dara-Abrams to think out loud about the characteristics of a great conversation; her rule is intended to create a context in which meeting participants can think expansively, learn from each other, and follow ideas and insights in new, unexpected directions. That is a far cry from the kind of meeting Parcell was describing.

Two different meetings with two different purposes and two different processes; there are no contradictions there that I can see.

So here is a different type of rule, perhaps the most important one I'll declare in this whole book: *There are No Absolute Rules; It All Depends.*

As you will see in more detail in Chapter 3, my overarching meeting model includes four components, and they interact with each other in delicate and complicated ways:

FIGURE 2.1

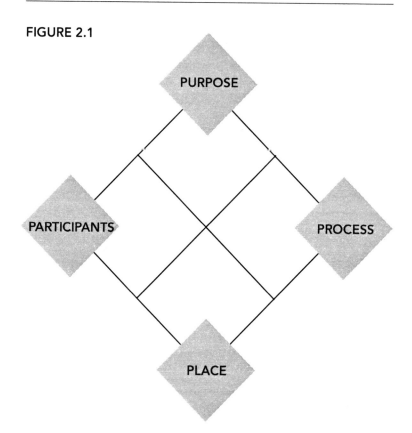

The Parcell and Dara-Abrams meetings clearly have different purposes, they require different processes (agendas, in combination with actual leadership behaviors), and they produce both different experiences and different results.

And that's okay. In fact, that's good. There is no simple formula for designing or leading effective meetings (and other kinds of conversations). That's where you come in. The essence of effective leadership is judgment: design and lead each of your conversations to accomplish your desired results.

If you can do that thoughtfully and consistently you will change the way you and your staff feel about your meetings. More than that, over time you'll change the culture of your organization.

And if you can create a culture where both results and experiences are valued, you'll affect both the bottom line and the employment line. Great work cultures produce great profits—and engaged employees.

A Brief Caveat about Leading Meetings that Matter

I am arguing strongly in favor of a collaborative style of leadership, and I believe that power-sharing and a "listen first" mindset is central to being an effective leader in today's networked economy. However, please understand that I am not advocating an "anything goes, any time, hands-off" approach.

As I will make clear in the coming chapters, a collaborative leader still has to lead: define your meeting's purpose; establish, and stick to, a clear agenda; and push for closure including resolution of outstanding decisions and/or problems. I'm calling for *a new kind of leadership*, not for any abdication of your leadership responsibilities.

Again, it's all about your mindset; act as a first among equals, not as a dictator or autocrat. Be respectful, listen to your colleagues, and focus on drawing out and leveraging their talents and ideas. *That's* what 21st-century leadership must be about.

Looking Ahead

Now it's time to get into the heart of the book. The next five chapters peel back the layers of meeting design and leadership. I take apart and explore in the detail the 4P meeting design framework depicted above in Figure 2.1, and then I offer a whole set of New Rules—and a few important tools—for ensuring that your meetings are both fun and productive.

Chapter Three

HOW CAN YOU DESIGN MEETINGS THAT MATTER?

T he first step in upgrading the quality of your meetings and other conversations is to be more intentional about them.

Because every one of us engages in work-related conversations of all kinds every day, it is highly unrealistic to suggest that you spend time thinking through every conversation before it takes place.

So let's focus on the most obvious ones—the formal meetings that are scheduled in advance—and seem to take place more than once every single day.

This chapter introduces a simple, basic model for thinking through the primary components of every conversation. It also lays out a taxonomy of meeting types, suggests criteria for determining who should participate in any particular meeting, and proposes a framework for understanding those participants and interpreting their responses during conversations.

The Four Parts of Every Conversation

I find it helpful to think of every conversation as having four separate components or dimensions: **Purpose**, **Participants**, **Process**, and **Place**, all of which are surrounded by a **Context** and preceded by **Preparation**, as shown in Figure 3.1.

FIGURE 3.1

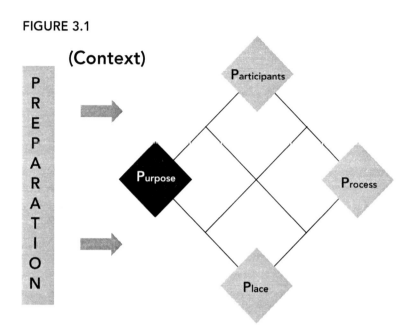

CONTEXT. What is the existing corporate culture? What are the norms and values that will filter what the participants in the meeting will hear and how they will react? Is the organization doing well financially, or are you in the middle of tough times? What performance pressures are employees feeling at the moment? Is the mood upbeat and optimistic, or stressful and depressing?

Your perspectives on these kinds of questions set the tone for your meeting and will guide your Preparation—which includes being clear about your Purpose, selecting which Participants you want in the meeting, defining your agenda, or Process, and selecting the Place where the meeting will occur.

PREPARATION. Every meeting (and every conversation, for that matter) consumes corporate resources—time and money. Don't walk into any meeting or significant conversation without thinking through all the variables and being clear about your purpose and expectations for the meeting.

What information will you share? What information do you want to learn? What decisions will be made? What commitments do you need, and from whom? How will you get to where you need to be?

Let's look first at those four corners of the "P" diamond:

- **Purpose.** Why are you calling the meeting? What are your desired outcomes? Is the conversation intended to exchange information, to change participants' minds about some issue or challenge, to inspire, or to move people to action? In Steven Covey's words, start with the end in mind.

- **Participants.** Who will you invite to participate in the meeting? Or, more appropriately, who should be participating? What are their talents, their learning styles? What do they know about each other? What are their roles and relationships? What do they already know and feel about the topic or the Purpose of the meeting?

- **Process.** What agenda will you follow to achieve the meeting's Purpose? What sequence of topics do you want to lead the group through? Who will lead each portion of the conversation? Will there be distinct phases to the meeting (e.g., information exchange, debate, decision-making)? Or will the conversation be more free-flowing? Will there be meeting minutes or other "products" generated during the meeting and shared afterwards?

- **Place.** Is the meeting face-to-face or is it distributed? What kind of space and furnishings will support your Purpose and desired Process? What technologies, if any, will be available to support communication and documentation of the conversation?

Whether any particular conversation is effective, and achieves your objectives, depends intimately on these four critical components and their interactions.

In the remainder of this chapter I will offer some ideas for thinking through your Purpose and understanding the Participants in advance of the meeting. Then in Chapter 4 I'll dig into how to manage the meeting's Process in some detail. I'll complete the model in Chapter 5, with a discussion of how Place impacts both a meeting's Process and its outcomes. Then, in Chapter 6 we'll consider how distributed meetings—when the participants are physically in different places—require particular kinds of leadership attention.

Purpose

With apologies to Gertrude Stein, a meeting is not a meeting is not a meeting.

There are at least ten distinct reasons or purposes for engaging in a conversation or holding a meeting. Of course any particular meeting may well have more than one purpose, and usually does. The important idea here is that these different purposes lead to different kinds of meetings:

- Informing (announcing, teaching)

- Sharing (exchanging information, experiences, ideas, opinions)

- Exploring (brainstorming, reviewing alternatives, combining ideas and experiences to create new insights)

- Planning (identifying possibilities and establishing intentions)

- Problem-Solving (moving from a problem to a solution)

- Designing (developing new concepts or new intentions)

- Producing (actually creating something, such as computer code or a marketing slogan)

- Decision-making (narrowing down from multiple alternative possibilities to a single choice)

- Persuading (changing the mindsets of some or all of the participants)

- Inspiring (appealing to peoples' emotions; motivating them towards new ways of thinking and/or acting)

Informational Meetings may be the most common type of group conversation in organizations today. Typically a team leader calls an informational meeting to announce news, to share decisions that have been made by more senior executives, or to inform staff about organizational changes, new products, new strategic messages, or any one of a number of other "facts" that the leader wants to share.

Sometimes there is also a teaching component; staff are informed about a new business process or procedure and then given new task responsibilities and even new jobs or roles resulting from the changes. The critical characteristic is that most of the information flow is one-way; there may be questions from the group, but the dominant purpose of the meeting is to provide participants with information that is new to them.

Sharing Meetings are more two-way; the goal is exchange ideas, insights, or other kinds of knowledge—information that comes from several different people rather than just from the team or meeting leader. A sharing meeting is characterized by more interaction, with many of the participants contributing to the conversation, either by offering specific perspectives or by asking questions of each other.

An **Exploring Meeting**, in contrast, has more of a brainstorming flavor, as participants seek to create new ideas or to build on each other's experiences to generate new perspectives that none of them had before the conversation began. At the end of an exploring meeting you want the participants to know more than when they began, including something about each other's ideas, insights, knowledge, or opinions

A **Planning Meeting** is designed to identify future opportunities or challenges along with ways the organization might want to respond to them. Planning meetings usually produce a plan or a series of action commitments and a list of possible future decisions or actions.

A **Problem-Solving Meeting** is convened to address some difficulty or challenge the organization is facing. For example, it might be about a process that is not producing the desired results, or a particular product deficiency that has become known through customer complaints, or perhaps a news article that reflects poorly on the company.

In an effective problem-solving conversation the group develops a common understanding of the problem or issue, builds a list of possible root causes, and then either agrees on the root cause or causes, or plans some future activities that will help determine how and why the problem arose. And of course a problem-solving meeting is incomplete unless the group identifies a solution that will potentially resolve the problem.

A **Design Meeting** is one in which the group generates specifications for a new product, a new process, a new database or information system, or something similar. It might flow directly out of a brainstorming or a problem-solving meeting, but it should produce tangible design specifications for the new product or process.

A **Production Meeting** is one in which actual work is accomplished; the product of the meeting could be some new software code, a new marketing slogan or brand image, or a new corporate policy. In contrast to the other kinds of meetings listed here, a production meeting goes beyond shared information, shared understanding, or increased knowledge; it actually relies on group collaboration to produce a tangible outcome.

Decision-Making Meetings are intended to produce group consensus about a future action that will be taken, or an issue that requires a choice.

A **Persuasion Meeting** involves some or all of the meeting participants changing their minds about something. Leading a persuasion meeting involves offering compelling reasons (both logical and emotional) for the meeting attendees to do something— which may or may not require changing their behaviors.

Inspirational Meetings do more than persuade; they affect the participants' deepest emotional states. They create motivation to do something specific, or to go beyond the ordinary to accomplish a goal that is shared by the group members.

Many, if not most, meetings have two or more of these purposes, and differing purposes do not necessarily require substantially different processes. However, the tone and "feel" of each type of meeting is usually distinctive.

[Not So] NEW RULE: Be clear about your purpose

I just described ten possible reasons for calling a meeting or having a conversation. But in all honesty that is just a suggestive list. What matters is that *you* are very clear about why you are calling *this* particular meeting. And that you communicate that purpose to everyone who you invite to participate.

Here are some guiding questions to help you make certain that each of your meetings is purposeful, effective, and productive.

First, ask yourself the most fundamental question of all: **Is this meeting necessary?**

As I have noted previously, a meeting is an expensive proposition. It consumes time for every participant—time they could use to do other work they are responsible for.

So why convene the meeting? I have already suggested a number of possible reasons, or purposes. But even if you have a legitimate goal of informing, influencing, or inspiring others, you still have to ask whether a *meeting*—whether in-person or virtual—is the most effective or most productive means of achieving that goal.

If you want to *inform* a group of people about a decision, a new strategy, or a new challenge, is a real-time face-to-face meeting the best way to do that? Why not prepare a memo or a white paper? Or send out a group e-mail? Or publish a public online document that everyone who needs to know can access online? With any kind of written communication all the recipients can read it and absorb its meaning at a time that is convenient for them. And they all read the same words—not an insignificant benefit.

However, the obvious downside of a written communication is that it is one-way, and there is no way for you to know if the recipients understand what you've said, or whether they agree with it. Or perhaps it raises questions in their minds that aren't addressed in the published document.

What happens then? There are two possibilities. First, some of the recipients may not voice their questions or concerns. In that case you won't know whether they understood the message and its intent until they do or say something that demonstrates their misunderstanding. And by then it may be too late to prevent a mistake or, worse, an unnecessary conflict.

Second, if they do raise a question or offer a different way of looking at the issue, then you will probably become involved in a lengthy string of one-to-one conversations (either verbal or written ones; both are time-consuming). Some people will pick up the phone and call you to discuss their questions in person. Some of those calls will probably go into your voice mailbox, triggering a time-consuming back-and-forth exchange that could go on for days before the two of you finally connect in real time.

Others will send you an e-mail; the same lengthy back-and-forth exchange will probably unfold. And e-mails take time to write, to read, and to respond to. Not only that, but if your e-mail correspondents use "Reply to All" as lots of people do, many people will be spending time reading and reacting to messages and information that may not be at all important to them.

So while on the surface a meeting may seem like a major time sink, it is often the most efficient way to pass information on to a group of people, and it may be the only way to ensure that they have all heard the same message and have developed a common understanding of its meaning.

A meeting can **potentially**—that's an important qualifier!— enable a group to gain accurate information more quickly and more completely than any other form of communication.

Furthermore, if your purpose is to persuade your team to support an idea, or change what they have been doing, or march off in a new direction with you, then a meeting is almost the only way to proceed.

Why? For the simple reason that unless you are a successful politician or an accomplished Hollywood actor, persuasion works best when it is embedded in a two-way conversation. There are some highly charismatic leaders and professional speakers who are very good at persuading large numbers of people from a convention hall platform or by speaking into a television camera, but frankly they are few and far between.

If you are focused on changing a group's mindset or actions, don't depend on a memo or an e-mail—especially if the change you are seeking is the least bit controversial or complex. If you want to persuade people to do something (or think something)—almost anything—differently than they are accustomed to, an interactive conversation is by far the most effective way to accomplish that goal.

Yes, you are bombarded every day with broadcast and printed advertisements by organizations that want you to buy toothpaste, or detergent, or weight-loss pills, or digital phones, or cars, gasoline, beer, and erectile-dysfunction pills. But those product companies have almost no other way to reach their millions of potential customers. The more they learn how to engage in two-way communication with those customers using the Internet and social media, the more they are moving away from one-way broadcast ads.

I've said before that the twenty-first century is the "Age of Networked Knowledge." And for me that means connecting in a *meaningful* way with others, whether you do it via e-mail, Twitter, Facebook, and other forms of social media, or by using plain, old-fashioned face-to-face conversations.

When you engage in a real-time two-way interaction you get immediate feedback, whether it is in the form of a direct challenge, a puzzled look, or a question.

You can then respond immediately to clarify a comment, correct a misunderstanding, or add additional information to make your case even more strongly. Or you can back up and restate your point of view, or turn the conversation around by asking questions yourself to help you understand the other participants' perspectives.

If your purpose is transformation or inspiration—building a new idea, a new outlook, a group commitment to new behaviors or values—then a new set of principles applies.

How else can individual perspectives or insights blend together into a shared understanding, or be combined in new and unforeseen ways?

Here are three basic principles to keep in mind when your Purpose is transformation or innovation:

- Open the meeting by emphasizing that you are seeking innovation, creativity, and new solutions—and there is no right or wrong answer.

- Launch a wide open search for ideas; and prevent any criticisms or outright dismissal of any ideas.

- State explicitly when it's time to move to a solution or develop consensus.

Participants

There are three basic questions to ask about the participants in any meeting you are responsible for:

- **Who do you want or need to be in the meeting?** Who are the stakeholders who will be affected by the meeting's outcome? Who has information, insight, or experience that is relevant and might affect the decisions or other meeting outcomes?

- **Who are the participants as individual human beings?** That is, what are their individual values, perspectives, talents, and experiences? What are their personal needs and objectives? What could they gain (or lose) as a result of their participation?

- **What are the participants' *organizational* roles?** What are their formal responsibilities? How are they measured and rewarded for their work? What kinds of personal and organizational pressures might they be feeling? What particular insights, needs, and perspectives will they bring to the conversation as a result of their organizational responsibilities and experiences?

I am not suggesting that you need to spend endless hours preparing for every meeting, but I want to encourage you to give these kinds of questions explicit attention as often as you can before you walk into that meeting room and launch the conversation.

You already know most of the answers to those kinds of questions. And as long as you have even a passing acquaintance with the people you are inviting to the meeting you'll be able to answer many of those questions immediately, or you'll know the answers in your gut.

Give explicit attention to everyone who will be involved in the conversation—who they are, what their perspectives are likely to be, what's in it for them, and how they can help you achieve your goals.

Now let's dig into those three questions a little deeper.

1. Who do you want to participate in the meeting?

Your choice of meeting participants depends, of course, on your Purpose and the required outcomes of the meeting.

Clearly you want to involve people in the meeting who have experiences and skills that relate to the meeting's Purpose. You also want to include at least some of those who will be affected by the outcomes of the meeting. If it's a decision affecting a budget or an action plan, then people whose resources will be enhanced, or reduced, should certainly be invited to participate.

If, on the other hand, the meeting is an exploratory or brainstorming meeting, then you want to invite people whose knowledge and experiences could potentially contribute to a positive outcome.

Give some thought to whether it is appropriate to include people from outside your immediate team—from other departments, for example. In every instance the key questions to ask yourself are:

- Who has the knowledge, expertise, and/or experience to contribute to the meeting's outcome?

- Who will be affected by the meeting outcome and will want an opportunity to influence that outcome, or at least to express his or her views about the outcome?

- Who will you need to carry out the decisions or plans that emerge from the meeting?

This is not to say that every single person who meets one of these criteria should be included. You obviously have to balance considerations about how critical an individual is to the meeting's success with other design issues like the size of the meeting, the meeting's importance to each participant relative to their other responsibilities, and any pre-existing opinions or relationship issues that could become barriers or blocks to a successful outcome.

One of the more difficult choices you have to make is whether to include potential naysayers in the meeting (or, more appropriately, when and how to deal with objectors and their objections).

This is particularly important if your Purpose is to persuade others to adopt a new point of view, to reach a decision on a controversial issue, or to brainstorm a new design that some may believe is unnecessary or even a bad idea.

Certainly one very effective way to win over objectors is to include them in the conversation; then even if you can't persuade them to change their minds, at least you have listened to them and made it impossible for them to complain that you ignored them. But including naysayers also risks giving them an opportunity to express their misgivings in public, and even to change the minds of people who currently support your position.

There are two dimensions to consider when you think about the stakeholders in any particular issue or decision: (1) are they with you or against you, and (2) how influential are they? Those two factors of course create four possible combinations, as depicted in Figure 3.2:

FIGURE 3.2

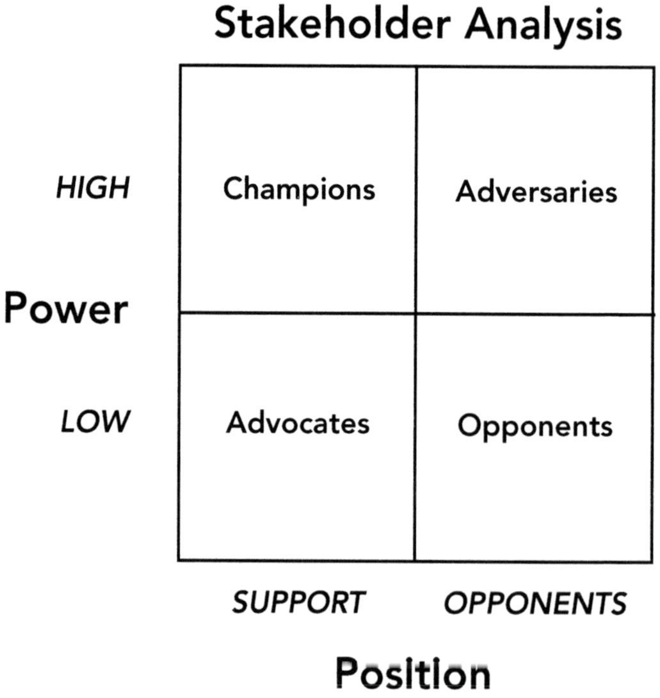

Stakeholder Analysis

	SUPPORT	OPPONENTS
HIGH	Champions	Adversaries
LOW	Advocates	Opponents

Power

Position

This Stakeholder Analysis tool is a simple but powerful framework for sorting out both who to include in your meeting and how to anticipate their likely positions on the issues.

Your assessment of how much power each stakeholder has (and how that power relates to your own) is critical. For example, if you have a very powerful adversary who opposes the meeting outcome you favor, you have to determine as accurately as you can whether that person can be won over, and if so by whom.

In contrast, you want to leverage your champions as much as possible. If your most powerful champion is a peer of, or has higher power than, your strongest adversary, ask for help in persuading the adversary either to change his or her position, or at least to minimize resistance.

You can follow the same influence strategy with advocates and opponents. Find influential advocates who can speak privately with opponents who are their peers or, preferably, less powerful.

By the way, I'm not suggesting that you should only try to achieve influence by using formal power and authority over those who oppose your ideas. In fact, sometimes you have to "speak up" and try to influence people whose organizational power is greater than yours. In those situations just remain aware of the differences in power and attempt to build a logically persuasive case for your position. In addition, try to identify ways in which your proposal will provide the other person or persons with organizational benefits that are important to them.

But it's even more complex than that. To the extent possible, be aware of the working and personal relationships among the various stakeholders. Putting organizational power differences aside, a friend will be listened to more carefully and more thoughtfully than will someone who the target hardly knows or cares about.

One final note about Participants: there is a powerful story about Steve Jobs, who was obviously a very powerful and charismatic leader. Jobs gave careful thought to meeting participation, both because he valued other people's time and because he was crystal clear about the outcomes he was seeking with every meeting.

The story is quite simple: as people were gathering for a meeting Jobs had called, one young woman he didn't know walked into the room. He asked who she was and why she was there. When she answered his questions, he responded along the lines of: "Thank you. There is really no need for you to be here; please excuse yourself." Jobs wasn't being elitist or arrogant; he was simply being practical.

Let's move on to the second question.

2. Who are the Participants as individual human beings?

There is nothing more important than knowing your staff and colleagues as human beings—who they are, what their work histories and experiences have been, what their current responsibilities are, what pressures they are experiencing, and what their personal talents and skills are (to say nothing of their personalities, quirks, and family situations).

Spend some time thinking about each of the potential Participants before you invite them. What are their assumptions—about you, about the problem or the opportunity the meeting will address, about the meeting's Purpose, about what will happen after the meeting? What is their personal frame of reference? That is, how will they interpret the meeting experience?

I first came across a deceptively simple three-part model for understanding someone's personal frame of reference when I was teaching at Harvard Business School over twenty-five years ago. Warning: it's simple in concept, but deeply profound in application.

Simply stated, our emotions, or **Feelings**, result from the intersection of our **Assumptions** and our **Perceptions**—the interplay between the way we believe things should be, and the way they are (or as we perceive them to be).

The meaning of any experience, including a conversation, comes from the interaction of those three components.

As Tony Athos and Jack Gabarro, two of my colleagues at Harvard, described it in their book *Interpersonal Behavior: Communication and Understanding in Relationships*:

> ". . . assumptions include all the beliefs, values, and attitudes that a person holds about how things are and how they ought to be . . . Assumptions are the . . . values that we incorporate into our conceptions of the world and into our conceptions of ourselves so that they become part of us."

Perceptions then are what we see or hear as actually taking place in our present world—or at least what we *think* we are seeing or hearing.

FIGURE 3.3

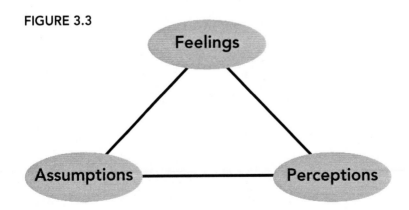

Athos and Gabarro observed that most personal and interpersonal problems come about when someone's (or two or more someone's) important assumptions are being challenged or contradicted by what they are currently hearing, seeing, or experiencing. It's the gap between "what should be" and "what is" that drives our emotions.

Given your understanding of the participants as individual human beings, what emotions and feelings do you expect each of them to bring to the meeting? Excitement? Curiosity? Skepticism about the outcomes? Satisfaction about being included? Resentment about the time the meeting will take? Any strong feelings that you can anticipate will help you prepare to deal with them and with whatever activity (or lack of activity) those feelings lead to during the meeting.

In addition, think through what work-related or personal issues each participant might be dealing with. If there are other projects, or deadlines, that are more important, they may well be feeling some resentment about having to attend the meeting, or at least some time pressure to get the meeting over with so they can return to their other priorities.

Finally, how can you leverage the positive feelings you anticipate they will bring? How can you head off any potential conflicts among the participants and deal with any negative feelings they may have about the topic or the meeting's purpose?

A Strengths-Based Framework for Understanding Others—and Yourself

Each of us approaches problems and relationships with a particular style, or from an individual point of view. There are dozens of personality and interpersonal style models (DISC, Myers-Briggs, and so on). Most of them differentiate people from one another along several dimensions that create a conceptual "map" or a set of "boxes" into which individuals can be sorted and lumped together.

For example, the widely-known Myers-Briggs model defines four dimensions that lead to sixteen different personality "types" as a way of describing people's behavioral and information-processing preferences.

That approach to understanding individual differences can be useful, but it also creates a serious risk of stereotyping other people. Management consultant Peter Bregman is deeply concerned that once you "know" someone's Myers-Briggs type (or DISC profile, or any other personality type), it becomes far too easy to stop seeing that person as a complex human being and to assume—falsely—that you know everything you need to know about him or her.

I share Bregman's concern; that is why I rely so much on the Assumptions-Perceptions-Feelings model described in the preceding section.

However, we all know that we do have individual tendencies, capabilities, and "styles" and that those styles clearly affect the way we react to ideas and to each other. Those differences, and the way we interact with other people, can certainly impact the way meetings and other conversations become either energizing or discouraging.

That said, there is one way of characterizing our individual differences that I do find compelling.

That model is based on the Clifton StrengthsFinder assessment, first defined by Marcus Buckingham and Donald O. Clifton of the Gallup Organization. Two of the many books describing their model and how to apply it are well worth getting and devouring: *Now, Discover Your Strengths* (Buckingham and Clifton) and *StrengthsQuest* (Clifton and Anderson).

The StrengthsFinder model identifies thirty-four talent themes that each of us has in varying degrees. More importantly, it assesses individual strengths and tendencies within each of those 34 dimensions, producing an individual talents profile.

The most important insight that Buckingham and his team brought to the search for peak performance was that each of us, and the teams we serve on, thrive far more when we focus on enhancing our strengths than we do when we spend time and effort trying to overcome our weaknesses.

Buckingham and his team at Gallup originally developed the talents model, but my good friend Candace Fitzpatrick, the founder and CEO of CoreClarity, Inc., has refined it and turned it into a powerful tool not just for identifying individual talents but for sorting out how the members of a team can most effectively work together to accomplish complex tasks.

Here is how Fitzpatrick describes her advocacy of a talents-based approach to team-building and collaboration:

> Contrary to old-school management philosophies, individuals, teams, and organizations excel by maximizing their strengths, not by fixing their weaknesses. Yet society is fixated on "fixing" people, trying to make them well-rounded so that they can fit in anywhere. The truth is we are all gifted in different ways, and trying to mold us into cookie-cutter shapes is contrary to our very nature.

The individual talent profiles that the CoreClarity team produces can help you understand who within your team are the thinkers, the planners, the learners, the achievers, the connectors, the doers, and the strategists (to name just of few of the roles that CoreClarity helps discern). Just think about the clarity that comes from knowing, for example, who is driven to take action, who is strongly empathetic, who can bring focus to a conversation, and who can keep the team directed towards the future.

Fitzpatrick likes to point out that the StrengthsFinder assessment produces more than 33 million different potential combinations of talents. Assume for just a moment that each one of those talent profiles is equally likely.

That means that in the United States, with a population of about 350 million people there may be only about ten or eleven other people with a profile exactly like yours. And when you add in age, gender, education, and regional cultures, there truly is only one of you.

The CoreClarity framework provides an incredibly powerful lens for looking at the way your team interacts and achieves results, both in meetings and in other work activities as well. That perspective is one of the major reasons I believe in a collaborative leadership style that values diversity rather than ignoring or destroying it, seeks ideas and insights from every possible source, and leverages the innate talents and unique perspectives of every individual team member.

The interaction of our differing talents and predispositions, in combination with our underlying assumptions and perceptions, has a direct effect on the tone and content of all our conversations.

Finally, be certain also that you know yourself as well as you know your team members. What are your talents, your shortcomings, your particular strengths and interests? What do you need and want from this meeting? How will its outcomes affect your future? Your reputation?

3. What are the participants' organizational roles?

In addition to knowing people as individual human beings, you must also be thoughtful about their organizational situations. What are they responsible for? How will their particular job responsibilities and pressures impact what they are willing (or unwilling) to contribute to the conversation and what they need out of it? Who do they report to, and what will they need to be able to tell their bosses and teammates about this particular meeting both before it takes place and after it is completed?

The functional or discipline-specific training that people bring to their organizational roles also affects the way they think and act in meetings. Perhaps the way someone thinks and acts—and has been educated—affects which organizational roles they gravitate towards or succeed at.

While I may be at some risk of stereotyping, just consider the difference in perspectives among HR, Technology, and Marketing professionals. People who have built careers in HR are likely to be people-oriented, sensitive to emotions and body language, and particularly focused on issues of fairness, equality, and thoughtful listening. In today's HR profession they are also likely to be literate about statistics, regulations, and compensation issues.

In contrast, IT professionals are highly focused on details, on achieving stable operations, and on technology as an end in itself. Marketing professionals are more likely to seek innovation and change, and to be aware of fashion, color, and both verbal and nonverbal communication patterns.

This is not the place to dig deeply into personality types or professional standards; but it is worth it for you to spend time thinking about how each meeting participant's functional responsibilities and expertise could impact his or her contributions and reactions in every meeting you prepare for.

Looking Ahead

Purpose and *Participants* are the two most important factors to think through before you schedule a meeting and invite anyone to it. But there are two other critical planning steps that should precede the actual meeting: developing your agenda—or, in the 4P model, planning the *Process*—and selecting where to hold the meeting—the *Place*.

Chapter 4 focuses on both designing and implementing the Process—how to plan out the experience that you want your meeting Participants to have, and then how to lead them through it. We'll then turn to the setting—the Place—in Chapter 5.

Chapter Four

LEADING MEETINGS THAT MATTER

N ow that I've identified how to prepare for your meeting, it's time to think through how to lead the actual conversation.

And while knowing *what* to do as a meeting leader is critical, I'm actually more focused on guiding you towards a *mindset* that views the meeting as an opportunity for learning, for engaging your staff, and for producing meaningful outcomes for your organization.

I begin by describing the core beliefs that characterize effective meeting leaders—the constructive mindset that is a precursor to being a constructive leader. Then I will walk you through the meeting experience, offering not so much a fixed menu of "How To's" but rather a smorgasbord of ideas, suggestions, and perspectives.

Do you remember that old military saying about how the battle plan goes out the window when you meet the enemy? I don't really want to compare meetings to military warfare (though they may sometimes feel like battles!), but obviously every meeting is unique, and most meetings that matter are fluid and dynamic. That is, you can't follow your script too closely or you risk sucking the life out of the conversation (remember that New Rule from Chapter 2: "Don't let a fixed agenda prevent a good conversation").

At the risk of horribly mixing metaphors, you might also want to think of a meeting as an improv performance; the most important mindset you can establish is to have a basic plan but then be "in the moment," reacting both instinctively and creatively to events as they evolve in real time. If there is one skill that matters most, it is the ability to think and respond quickly as a conversation unfolds.

Be willing to guide the conversation and keep it on track, but do that as loosely as you can, while maintaining order and staying focused on achieving your Purpose.

Adopt a Constructive Mindset

As I suggested in Chapter 2, the most significant thing you can do as a meeting leader to ensure that any particular conversation is meaningful is to approach it with a positive, growth-oriented mindset. For me that includes several critical New Rules, many of which are not really new but are often forgotten in the middle of a conversation:

- **Assume that the group is far more intelligent and experienced than any single participant.** Remember, no one individually is smarter than everyone together. And that includes you!

- **Presume that people can learn and grow.** And that also includes you. Be open to learning from anyone about anything. Remember that you are already in a position of leadership; you don't have to prove that you are smarter or better informed than the other participants. In fact, going out of your way to demonstrate how much you know is a sure way to lose the respect of everyone else in the meeting.

- **Focus on broad goals that everyone agrees with.** Start the conversation with common goals and seek win/win solutions whenever possible.

- **Respect individual differences.** Remember that there is only one of you, and there is only one of everybody else in the world. I've highlighted several times already the synergy that's possible when you draw out those differences. It's not only individual experiences and knowledge that are different; just as important are the distinctive talents, and the individual ways of processing information and responding to other people, that each person brings to the conversation.

- **Be mindful of others' responsibilities, constraints, and needs.** Unless you believe it is unavoidable, don't ask the meeting participants to make commitments or agree with positions that will make their own lives more difficult. Respecting their individual circumstances includes avoiding putting them into difficult positions or endangering their personal and professional relationships.

- **Suspend judgment.** Hear people out and be sure you understand their ideas in sufficient depth before you decide (and certainly before you communicate) whether those ideas are useful and relevant, or a distraction.

- **Enter every conversation with an open and curious mind.** You just never know what experiences and relevant knowledge the other participant(s) might bring to the conversation.

- **Look for common ground.** Find areas of agreement, or at least where the participants' insights overlap. Build on that sense of commonality to move towards consensus, or at least to find something that everyone can agree on. Once you've established that common ground it will be much easier (and less stressful) to explore areas of disagreement.

- **Be authentic.** Admit it when you don't know an answer, or need help. Express the emotions you are experiencing;

for example, if someone comes up with an exciting and innovative idea, thank them or praise them (but only if you genuinely mean it). Or if you are confused or can't follow someone's train of thought, say so (in a caring and respectful way, of course).

- **Reinforce constructive behaviors from others.** When someone else offers thanks, or praise, thank them in turn. Reward behaviors that help move the conversation forward, and over time you will see more of them.

- **Know where you are in the process, and let others know as well.** Presumably you defined the meeting agenda, and told the other participants how you want the conversation to unfold. If you ignore that agenda, or go off topic, you are implicitly giving everyone else permission to do the same thing. That makes it much more difficult to rope someone else in when they've gone off on a tangent.

If there is one aspect of meeting leadership where Command and Control still fits, it is in keeping the group on track as you guide it through the agenda. Do it with a firm but flexible style; the image of an iron fist inside a velvet glove is a good one to remember.

But First, Let the Meeting Start by Itself

There's nothing small about small talk.

In western economies it has almost become a cultural norm to spend the first five or ten minutes of a formal meeting engaging with the other meeting participants in what we call "small talk." You know, those pre-call-to-order conversations that seem to just happen as people arrive in the meeting room—conversations that begin with questions and comments like:

- "How was your weekend?'

- "What are your kids up to?

- "Man, it's way too hot this summer!" or, "Can you believe how cold it was last night!"

- "Congratulations! I just heard about your daughter's gymnastics victory last night."

- "Hey, I just heard that Freddie in marketing got a big promotion because of that killer ad campaign he designed."

Most of us think of those topics as trivial, and primarily a way to kill time until everyone arrives and the "real" meeting starts. And yes, they do help occupy people's minds until the host calls the meeting to order. But they can also make or break the "real meeting" that follows.

Sometimes the informal chatter that emerges out of "small talk" questions goes on for fifteen or twenty minutes. It is fascinating how engaged people can become with "everyday" topics like the weather, their families, local sports teams, company gossip, and even politics (but only if the group generally leans towards the same end of the political spectrum!).

Small talk is a powerful way of connecting people to each other as human beings, not just as some abstract person doing some abstract job.

Small talk is the way we learn about each other's lives outside of work (and sometimes inside as well, when the small talk turns to office gossip, or to more legitimate news of company events, sales successes, and other important work-related activities).

Whenever I work with the managers of remote employees and telecommuters, I always encourage them to begin every conference call with a few moments of exactly this kind of small talk. It not only helps identify who is on the call, but it helps everyone (not just the manager or call host) get a sense of the participants' current state of mind—and that's useful knowledge as you begin to focus on the meeting topics and face difficult issues and decisions.

Small talk is really a big thing.

In fact, Patt Schwab, founder of FUNdamentally Speaking, believes that small talk does a whole lot more than just connect people with each other (as important as those connections are). She spent many years in academic environments, managing college student housing facilities and staff, and leading hundreds of meetings herself.

I recently asked Schwab what she thinks makes a good conversation. Her first response was "respect for the other person." She then went on to talk about how important it is for all the participants to be "in the moment."

All that makes plenty of good sense, but Schwab then really made me think when she talked about the impact of *intentionally* opening meetings with several minutes of "small talk"—especially for "standing" meetings like weekly staff update sessions, where there is often very little energy, and usually no explicit agenda or particular issue that captivates the attendees or focuses their attention.

Remember how much Sue Bingham's staff enjoyed those Monday morning status meetings when they began with "movie reviews" that encouraged her staff to share their weekend experiences?

Staff members typically show up in the conference room for those weekly meetings with their heads full of concerns about all the unfinished work piled up on their desk, or with children who are sick at home, or struggling to pass geometry, or wrapped up in friendships that are deteriorating.

In Schwab's view, the value of informal chatting and storytelling as people are arriving at those meetings is not just it that helps them connect to each other's lives (which it clearly does)—but also that it brings them into the moment, perhaps distracting them from all those personal concerns and helping them be ready to focus on the task at hand, or at least on the other people in the room.

I believe the most important factor that drives a conversation from good to great is that each participant genuinely wants to learn from the other person, and small talk is a way of opening us up to learning what's going on in other people's lives.

Or Start with No Talk at All

60 Minutes carried a story on Mindfulness reported by Anderson Cooper, who has embraced the core concepts of mindfulness over the past several years. After a lengthy exploration of how mindfulness, meditation, and other "centering" techniques help many people reduce stress and regain control of their lives, Cooper concluded his report by interviewing Karen May, Vice President of People Development at Google.

May told Cooper that Google has offered mindfulness training and meditation classes to many of its employees, and that the company has even hired a full-time "Jolly Good Fellow" (that's his job title; he is a former Google software engineer named Chade-Meng Tan) as part of the company's emphasis on employee well-being. Mr. Chade-Meng leads training classes and workshops designed to help employees develop a better sense of balance in their lives.

One manifestation of this focus on well-being at Google is to begin meetings with several minutes of silence. That has become a "pause that refreshes" in that it encourages meeting participants to take a few deep breaths, think about the meeting that is about to begin, and clear their minds of other concerns, other projects and deadlines, and everything else that could distract them from the meeting at hand. It's a powerful way of being "in the moment," one of the key tenets of the Mindfulness movement.

Blogger Conor Neill reports that Amazon has taken the idea of moments of silence even further. CEO Jeff Bezos realized that depending on PowerPoint presentations "makes it easy on the presenter and hard on the audience" because that style of information sharing relies on bullet points and very little meaningful data (remember also Alice Dee's story in Chapter 2 about meetings filled with stories rather than PowerPoint slides)

Not only that, but as adult-learning expert Stephen Campbell points out in *Making Your Mind Magnificent*, we think at least three times faster than we listen; our minds wander and we tend to get bored very quickly listening to a one-way presentation.

Add that to the fact that almost no one has time to read pre-meeting briefing documents before they arrive at a meeting, and some Amazon team leaders now begin their meetings by asking everyone to sit silently for up to thirty minutes as they read a six-page narrative briefing document on their own.

At Amazon, the actual meeting conversation begins only when everyone has read the document in question individually and has had time to reflect on it and form opinions and/or questions. Then, and only then, does the conversation begin.

Leading the Meeting Experience

With those core principles and examples as context, here are several additional questions and more New Rules for conducting your conversations effectively.

NEW RULE: Model the tone you want to see

Some meetings are somber, serious discussions of challenging issues or important information; they often require tough decisions with difficult compromises and trade-offs. Others, as noted earlier, are intended to stimulate brainstorming and creativity. If you want a light-hearted tone, start off with a joke, or some tongue-in-cheek observation about the group, the company, or the news of the day. If you need a more serious, focused meeting, get right down to business by opening with the agenda and your objectives for the meeting.

NEW RULE: Start the meeting with a check-in

It is almost always useful to convene the meeting by asking each Participant to "check-in" by describing their individual state of mind and their hopes/expectations for the meeting. In addition, ask if there is anything particularly important going on in their lives that they want to share with the others. This request often leads to surprising stories about personal successes or challenges (an anniversary, a birthday, a child's success at school, a spouse's recent promotion—or a family illness, the loss of a pet, a local community issue, or even a death or divorce).

To the extent that Participants are willing to share such personal news, and are in the habit of raising those kinds of celebrations and concerns, the meeting is more likely to evolve smoothly, or it might take a different direction than you had planned—which can be either good or bad, depending on your goals for the meeting.

NEW RULE: Ensure that everyone feels comfortable expressing their points of view and accepts others' perspectives as LEGITIMATE

It is almost always appropriate to open a meeting by first stating the meeting's purpose and desired outcomes, and then reminding the participants of the "rules" of a good conversation. I like to ask a group to think out loud for a few moments about what will make the meeting a good one from their perspective, and also what anyone in the room could do to sabotage the meeting. That is, what kinds of behaviors could get in the way of achieving the meeting's goals?

That approach accomplishes several things: it sets an expectation of widespread participation; it establishes that everyone's ideas are valid; and it puts the onus for avoiding counterproductive behaviors on the participants themselves—after all, they have just identified those behaviors as unacceptable or destructive. Having those ideas out in the open makes it easy for you to "call out" someone when they do anything counterproductive during the meeting.

NEW RULE: Tolerate uncertainty and differing perspectives as long as possible

Our most important work in organizations is focused on solving problems and/or producing new ideas—product designs, marketing campaigns, new ways of understanding why sales are growing or shrinking, cheaper ways of operating the business.

However, I sometimes think the biggest barrier to effective brainstorming and problem-solving is the tendency most groups have to close in on a solution too quickly. Most people have a low tolerance for uncertainty and ambiguity; it can be highly stressful to experience a gap between where the group is and where someone wants or needs it to be. Understandably, we want to develop a solution as quickly as possible in order to reduce that stress. However, the more widely you search for an answer the more likely you are to discover (or invent) an effective solution.

In fact, many groups are guilty of what has been called the "streetlight effect." Behavioral scientist Abraham Kaplan described this effect in his 1964 book *The Conduct of Inquiry* as the "principle of the drunkard's search."

The story has been told in many different variations, but it usually goes something like this:

> A policeman encounters an old man, clearly drunk, wandering around in circles under a streetlight. "What's the matter?" says the policeman. "I dropped my car keys," says the drunk. After several minutes of searching with him, the policeman asks "Are you sure you lost them here?" The drunk replies, "No, I lost them over there, in the park." When the policeman asks why he is looking for them at the street corner, the drunk replies, "It's a lot easier to see here."

In other words, most groups don't search widely enough, or long enough, or in the right "places" for creative solutions; they focus on the easy and familiar ideas they already know. They can't handle the stress of not knowing what their ultimate decision and actions might be.

It is useful to think of problem-solving in two phases: first a wide, *divergent* search for ideas that might be useful, without any attempt to resolve the problem; and then a second, *convergent* phase that focuses on selecting the best solution from among all the ideas that were discovered earlier on. As I've already suggested, the wider the divergent search the higher quality the final solution is likely to be.

I like to picture the process like this:

FIGURE 4.1

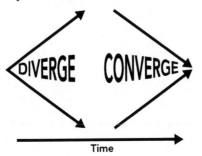

Note two things: first, the longer the two diverging arrows on the left are, the wider the search for a solution will be. Second, although this picture implies equal time spent on each activity, there is no requirement that the time spent on the two steps be identical. A group searching for a breakthrough solution might spend four hours brainstorming, but then be so clear about the value of the new insights it has discovered that it takes less than thirty minutes to select the best solution and build unanimous support for it.

One more note about divergent thinking: the more diverse the contributors are, the more likely you're going to come up with something truly new and innovative. Patt Schwab told me recently that one large high-tech company she knows has hired into one of its product design teams not only systems analysts and software programmers but also a classical musician and a professional hockey player. Why? Different perspectives and different insights into what consumers want. Divergent thinking thrives with diverse input.

NEW RULE: Demand, and demonstrate, respect for all points of view

Mutual respect is the *sine qua non* of effective conversations. As I have pointed out several times, the most valuable asset of any team or organization is the diversity of its members. Each participant brings a unique set of skills and experiences to the group, and that's what ensures that no one is smarter than everyone—but only if those diverse experiences, ideas, and insights all have a chance to be heard.

NEW RULE: Listen to understand, not to judge

If you accept the idea that a conversational leader's role is to sense and guide, then pay very close attention to what every participant is saying, and what emotions they are expressing. But be certain that you are listening for understanding, not to judge or evaluate what is being said.

As conversation expert Judith Glaser explains,

> When we listen to connect we open and expand the space, allowing [the speakers'] aspirational [selves] to emerge. [When] we think out loud with them, and share our dreams with them and co-create with them we all experience ourselves in a new way.

Ask penetrating, open-ended questions, and add follow-up questions that extend your understanding. In the back of your mind you might question the validity of a statement, or be upset about a negative tone of voice. But remember that as the meeting leader you want to create an environment where everyone feels safe and free to express themselves, no matter what the content of their message (within the bounds of civility, of course).

So even if you are personally skeptical or even upset with what you're hearing, ask questions that deepen the group's understanding of what's being said. And remember that you are probably not the only one who feels skeptical or upset; often one of the other participants will confront the speaker and deal with the issue before you need to say anything.

It is important for you as the leader to model appropriate ways to respond to controversial statements or emotional outbursts; while it may be difficult to remain calm, it is critical if you want to avoid having the meeting degenerate into a chaotic argument. Listening for understanding rather than being judgmental does not mean anything goes. Disagreeing without confronting is not easy, but it is central to keeping things on track.

NEW RULE: Listen for meaning

The next time you are in a meeting, listen for the meaning behind the words, and seek out what that deeper meaning can bring to the challenges at hand. The best way I know to sort out what any idea or comment means to someone else is to ask yourself, as I suggested in Chapter 3, what is their frame of reference?

Remember that an individual frame of reference consists of three components: *Assumptions*, *Perceptions*, and *Feelings*. Feelings, or emotions, result from the interplay between our **assumptions** about the way the world works, and—more importantly—the way we believe it *should* work on the one hand, and our **perceptions** about what we believe is actually happening, on the other.

The next time you see a meeting participant getting tight-lipped and red in the face, ask yourself what that person must be assuming or wishing for that is in conflict with what is happening or being said at the moment. In the vernacular, pay attention to where they're coming from, and you'll understand a lot more about where they're trying to go.

NEW RULE: Ask open-ended questions

I've also become convinced that meaningful conversations start with thoughtful questions. A question signals your interest in learning—your openness to new information and new ideas.

Remember that your role—and your goal—as a conversation leader is to draw out and blend the ideas, insights, and experiences of everyone involved in the conversation. By far the most effective way of achieving that goal is to ask questions that encourage participants to share their insights and ideas, and to respond to their colleagues thoughtfully and respectfully.

There are two basic types of questions: **closed-ended** and **open-ended**. Each type has its place in conversations. But they have very different consequences.

A closed-ended question asks for a specific bit of information; it can be answered with a yes or a no, or with a specific piece of information. Yes/no questions are usually requests for information, such as:

- "Did you finish that report on last month's budget deficit?"

- "Have you met the new Regional Sales Director?"

- "Have you seen our competitor's new national ad campaign?"

Some closed-ended questions are not yes/no in nature, but they are equally focused on a specific bit of information:

- "What time are you meeting with Bob tomorrow?"

- "How much did the XYZ widget sales grow over the last six months?"

- "How far is Grand Forks from Omaha?"

Those kinds of questions do not typically invite further discussion; they signal a desire for information, not a conversation. In fact, all too often they have the effect, either intentionally or unintentionally, of shutting down either the entire conversation or an individual participant.

In the worst case, closed-ended questions are accompanied by a tone of voice that conveys sarcasm, arrogance, or an emotional message like "I already know the answer to my question; I want to be sure you do too." Consider questions like these (and imagine you are hearing them in that know-it-all tone of voice):

- "Did you see the way Bob sneered when he told Jane to get her act together?"

- "Do you *really* believe our sales are going to go up by 25 percent in the next two months?"

- "Do you really think *you* are the most qualified software engineer in the company?"

In fact, when used this way, a "question" isn't really a request for information at all; it's a statement (and usually a negative one at that) masquerading as a question.

In contrast, an open-ended question asks the responder to offer an idea, a hypothesis, or even a guess about the topic, or it requests more detail about something that has already been mentioned.

For instance, if someone has just suggested that the company open a new office in downtown Boise, Idaho, you could respond with a shut-down question by saying something like "Why would we want to do that?" That kind of question isn't likely to expand the conversation because it's so obviously a challenge. The unspoken message is something like "You don't know what you are talking about."

A more genuine, supportive way of following up on the suggestion about opening that office in Boise might be to ask something like: "What benefits do you see that producing?" That's an open-ended question in that there are many possible answers (some of which may actually be interesting and new for you).

Open-ended questions that are asked with a sincere interest in the answer serve to:

- Express respect for the other person (you are presuming that he/she has more useful information).

- Offer an opportunity for the other person to add more information, thereby enhancing the conversation.

- Demonstrate your interest in the topic.

- Convey your desire to keep the conversation going.

■ Stimulate more questions from other participants.

The other advantage of using open-ended questions is that you are putting the responsibility for responding on the person you are directing the question to but doing so in a respectful way that conveys your genuine interest in the response.

NEW RULE: Ask follow-up questions to extend and deepen the conversation

Open-ended questions almost by definition dig deeper into a topic by encouraging additional comments. And they leave the direction of the conversation up to the speaker—the person you have directed the question to.

In my experience, the first time many ideas are expressed in a meeting they are often incomplete, or so vague that they leave lots of room for interpretation and potential misunderstanding. One of the most important tasks of a meeting leader or facilitator is to clarify what's been said by asking the speaker to expand on the original comment, or to add important details.

For example, if someone says: "Why don't we add a Frequently Asked Questions section to our customer support website?" You could respond with something like: "What kinds of information do you think we should include?"

Or: "How would that help our customers? (Be sure your tone of voice conveys genuine interest, not a skeptical challenge to the concept)

Or: "Do you think a FAQ section could reduce the number of calls on our 800 customer service number?"

I'm not suggesting that you pepper the other person with all three of those questions one after another; rather, each of them could be a follow-up either to the original idea or to further comments as the conversation unfolds.

Often these kinds of questions actually help the other person think more deeply about his or her idea; having to expand on the first statement creates an opportunity to think out loud and extend the idea.

Unless the original comment produces an obvious, clear, and straightforward next step, the group is going to need more details before it can make a decision or a commitment to future action.

One of a meeting leader's primary responsibilities is to draw out to the greatest extent possible all the ideas and information that emerge during the conversation.

But that does not mean the meeting should be a sequence of leader/respondent two-person conversations. One of the most effective things a conversation leader can do is to foster conversations that engage several, if not all, of the meeting participants.

One of the techniques that I learned early in my career as a case study teacher at Harvard Business School was to ask my students to comment on each other's comments. Then, if there was a disagreement, or different ideas were surfacing, I could ask them to respond to each other, or even ask a third person to comment on the difference in perspectives. If I wanted to be confrontational I might even ask Joe whether he agreed with Mary or with Bob—or which one of their comments was correct.

However, there is rarely any long-term value in being that direct. Remember that the purpose of most meetings is to build common understanding or to resolve a conflict or make a decision about some future action.

For those goals you want the participants to feel good about each other and the topic. Engineering a confrontational debate and generating ill will among the participants rarely moves the group in that direction. Your role as a leader is to sense and to guide; to sense where the conversation is while knowing where it needs to go next, and then guiding it in that direction.

Be clear in your own mind about whether the topic calls for more divergent and creative thinking, or if it is time for convergence—narrowing the focus and reaching a decision. Your questions and structuring comments should then reflect your responsibility for moving the conversation forward.

NEW RULE: You are a role model

One of the most powerful effects that a meeting leader can have on a conversation is that of serving as a role model who acts out a specific example of how to respond respectfully in ways that move the conversation forward.

As the corporate conversations I participate in unfold, it is remarkable how often I see the participants mimicking the leader. They ask the same kinds of questions, they copy the leader's tone of voice, and they often pursue a line of reasoning that clearly follows and sometimes even anticipates the direction the leader is taking the group.

Leadership Interventions

There are at least three distinct kinds of leadership interventions that help make a meeting constructive:

- Structuring comments
- Guiding comments
- Pointing out the elephant comments

Structuring Comments

The leader's role—understood and accepted by just about

everyone who ever attended a meeting—is to open a meeting with a statement about its purpose and intended outcomes. The most important thing you can do next is to describe the path forward—in other words, tell the group how you envision the conversation evolving from where you are to where you want to be.

But the beginning of the meeting isn't the only time to insert structure. It is also your responsibility to keep the conversation on track—without being overly controlling or dictatorial. You should always have a rough timeline in mind—how long to spend on opening comments, helping the group understand and accept its task; how long to engage in brainstorming or exploring the issues; how long to allow for the group to reach consensus or come to a decision; and how long to "debrief" and confirm follow-up action commitments once the required decisions have been made.

When I am particularly concerned about covering all the agenda items for an upcoming meeting I sometimes write out a "storyboard" that includes each major phase of the meeting as I envision it, along with an approximate time block for each item. A storyboard is a cool tool that enables me to test whether the meeting is doable, and to develop a clear understanding of when it will be time to bring each phase to a close and move on.

Keep an eye on the clock, and provide "gentle" reminders as often as needed. It is your role, and your prerogative, as leader to decide when "enough is enough"—when it's time to close debate on an issue, or when the comments are getting to be repetitious or superfluous.

In my experience many group leaders and even skilled facilitators are often a bit tardy in moving the group on to the next topic; the participants often recognize the need to get back on track before the group leader does, even if they are reluctant to take responsibility themselves for moving the conversation forward.

Guiding Comments

When a meeting leader makes a "gentle" suggestion or a subtle observation about either the content of the conversation or the process itself, I consider those to be guiding comments rather than structuring ones. Your tone of voice and the words you choose convey your intentions and how serious you are to the other participants.

Consider the difference between these two different comments:

"We've spent enough time on the market segmentation data; let's move on to the product quality feedback that's coming from each of those segments."

"Alan, that's a very helpful way to sort out who our customers are, but I think we'd learn more if we could focus now on what they are actually saying about our product."

These two interventions generally serve the same ultimate purpose; they suggest the group has spent enough time on market segmentation and would be better served by turning to more specific product quality feedback.

But note how different their tone is; the first comment is basically a formal leadership intervention—what I call a Structuring Comment—while the second is a more gentle "nudge" to move forward.

I am not suggesting that one or the other of these approaches is universally better or more effective. Your choice and the impact of the intervention will depend on several factors, including your relationship with the group, the importance of the topic, and how far along the group is on this meeting's agenda.

Pointing out the Elephants in the Room

One of the more difficult—but critically important—roles of a meeting leader is to bring unstated comments or feelings out into the open: that is, to express the issues that everyone in the room knows are impacting the conversation but no one seems willing to talk about.

The so-called "elephant in the room" is an issue that is lurking under the surface, or a concern or question that all the participants are most likely thinking about but no one is expressing out loud.

Those elephants can easily sidetrack an otherwise productive meeting. For example, if there are rumors afloat about someone being terminated, or a bad quarterly earnings report, or a new corporate benefits program, participants' unspoken questions about those rumors could dominate their thoughts and block any efforts the leader might make to foster an open, exploratory brainstorming meeting or a decision about a divisional product strategy that might be directly affected by that rumor.

Of course, you as the responsible meeting leader may well have no more information than anyone else in the room about that particular issue. But if that is the case, the least you can do is to make a statement something like this:

> You've all been hearing rumors about our quarterly earnings report. I know we are all concerned, but unfortunately at this point I don't know any more than the rest of you. So let's put that uncertainty aside for the time being and focus in on our new product launch strategy. I promise I will let you know about the earnings as soon as I hear from the CFO.

With that statement you've acknowledged the issue everyone is concerned about, and even though you can't resolve it, you've assured the participants that you will share the report with them as soon as you have access to it. That may not fully resolve the tensions in the room, but by making those tensions visible and telling everyone it is "okay" to be feeling that way, you have asked them to put the concern aside for the time being and get back to the meeting's purpose and agenda.

There's a wonderful story about a domineering CEO who was frustrated at how passive his leadership team was during their planning meetings. Then, on a particularly frustrating day, Tom, the Chief Financial Officer, became so frustrated with the way the CEO cut someone else off that he blurted out "Why are you treating David like s**t? He's only trying to help."

Taken aback the CEO replied, "I'll decide what I want to say and when I want to say it. You shouldn't have said that."

To which Tom replied, "Well, you're right about one thing. I shouldn't have said that."

At which point the whole team burst out laughing at Tom's remorse. Even the CEO had to smile, and then to acknowledge that he was being unfair. From that point forward the team found it much easier to be open about their feelings and the conversation process they were engaged in. And over time even the CEO relaxed and learned to listen more nonjudgmentally.

Sometimes all it takes is someone to point out that the emperor has no clothes, or that an unacknowledged elephant is stifling progress.

Facilitation versus Formal Leadership

In most meetings the leader plays at least two formal roles. One is defining the meeting's purpose and agenda and paying close attention to both the information and the emotions that are relevant to the meeting's outcomes.

The other role is leading the conversation process, paying attention as noted earlier to progress through the defined agenda; drawing out ideas and insights from all the participants; ensuring that they confront their differences in ways that enhance the conversation, not destroy it; and finally bringing the meeting to a close and a conclusion.

Those two roles are actually quite different, and they require different, although complementary, skills. They also require different kinds of "acceptance" from the rest of the participants. In most cases the meeting leader is the most senior person in the room in a hierarchical sense (there are occasions when the meeting leader is not the highest-level person present, but those are special cases).

Most organizational leaders are understandably much clearer about their formal authority planning and leadership role than they are about the process-oriented or facilitation role. I have worked with several organizations where those two roles are recognized as distinct; and most leaders who understand the distinction recruit a separate meeting facilitator to help ensure that the meeting runs smoothly and accomplishes its purposes.

Separating the two roles and embedding them in two different people can be incredibly useful. First, it enables the formal leader to inject his knowledge and experience into the conversation without having to worry about the agenda, or the timing, or achieving the meeting's goals. Those responsibilities are in the hands of the facilitator.

A facilitator can act as a time-keeper, referee, and conversation-enabler. However, an effective facilitator never forgets who is ultimately in charge of the meeting. A skilled facilitator always acknowledges where the power in the room resides; he offers suggestions, makes observations, and confronts issues thoughtfully and even humbly.

A facilitator exercises influence through expertise, not authority. A facilitator becomes effective when helping to move the group along to its intended destination. A facilitator's concern must be with the candor and inclusiveness of the conversation, not with any particular conclusion or direction it takes.

More New Rules: Principles for Facilitators

There are many books and formal course programs on how to become an effective meeting facilitator. I have listed several books and other resources that I consider useful in the Resources and Notes section.

Here I just want to suggest a few basic operating principles that any team or meeting leader should be aware of. However, please view these as guidelines, not prescriptions or even New Rules.

The most important attribute of a skilled facilitator is judgment— that "sixth sense" about when to intervene, when to raise unspoken issues or emotions, and when to be tentative versus definitive about a particular observation or suggestion.

If you are a formal team or meeting leader working with a facilitator, look for someone who puts these principles into practice:

- **Focus on the process, not the content, of the conversation.** A facilitator is charged with ensuring that the conversation flows smoothly, that all points of view get a fair hearing, and that issues are confronted adequately as well as civilly. The direction of the conversation, and any conclusions or decisions that the group comes to, remain the responsibility of the formal group or meeting leader.

- **Listen to feelings, and be prepared to express them.** One of the most constructive things a facilitator can do is to give voice to the emotions that are "under the surface" in the conversation—especially if they are strong or negative emotions. Be sensitive to tone of voice, and to words and phrases that may have special meaning within this particular team.

- **Express observations, perceptions, and hypotheses, not opinions or conclusions.** Almost everything a facilitator says should be perceived by the group as a tentative idea or insight, being expressed as something for the group to consider, not as a "take it or leave it" assertion. A facilitator's acceptance within a group has to be earned, and it comes from being insightful more often than being disruptive or confrontational.

NEW RULE: Close the meeting with a "check-out"

Just as you opened the meeting with a check-in that gives all the participants a chance to describe their current state of mind and express their hopes and concerns about the meeting, a "check-out" offers them a parallel opportunity to share their assessments of how well the meeting went and whether or not it achieved its Purpose.

The check-out gives you as the meeting leader a good "read" on how the Participants experienced the meeting, and what level of understanding they have of the just-completed conversation. Perhaps even more importantly, it can tell you a great deal about how engaged they were, how committed they are to the decisions just made, and what issues to be concerned about going forward.

There are many ways to initiate a checkout round. Here are three:

- "Okay, as we wind up, let's go around the room for a quick checkout. How are you feeling about our conversation? What are you ready to do next?"

- "Okay everyone, thank you for your time and your ideas. Let's go around quickly—one minute max per person. What is the most important idea you picked up today? What could we do next time to make the conversation even more productive?"

- "Thank you for your time and your input today. How are you feeling right now? What questions remain for you about our decision? What do you intend to do to make sure we carry out our commitments?"

At the end of every one his meetings my good friend Jim Horan likes to ask his clients what they expect or intend to do differently as a result of their conversation. That's another useful technique for soliciting feedback about whether the meeting achieved your goals.

Note that some check-out comments could invite another whole round of debate and discussion. If it becomes obvious that the issues you thought were resolved are still alive, you either have to confront them right then and there, or commit to pick them up at a future meeting. But it's certainly preferable to have that information right then rather than discover it only much later.

NEW RULE: It's not over when it's over

Every meeting should be followed by an After-Action Review.

The "After-Action Review" (AAR) was first developed and implemented by the U.S. Army in the 1970s. It has become standard operating procedure for U.S. military teams to conduct formal reviews after both training exercises and actual operational maneuvers.

Here is a description of the AAR approach from the Knowledge Sharing Toolkit wiki website (originally developed by the Global Agricultural Research Partnership):

- AARs should be carried out with an open spirit and no intent to blame. The American Army used the phrase "leave your rank at the door" to optimize learning in this process. Some groups document the review results; others prefer to emphasize the no-blame culture by having no written record.

- AAR is a form of group reflection; participants review **what** was intended, **what** actually happened, **why** it happened and what was learned.

One of the military AAR procedures that seems particularly important to me is to begin each review by asking the most junior person in the group to reflect on and critique the just-completed activity.

That practice protects junior staff from having either to disagree actively with their organizational superiors, or to remain quiet to avoid being seen as insubordinate. To the Army's credit it recognizes the reality of power and career pressures within its hierarchy.

I sometimes wish we could just eliminate all power/authority differentials in organizations, but we know that's impossible, nor is it appropriate. Realistically, however, the cost of disagreeing is usually much higher for junior staff than it is for people in more senior, more secure positions. The key to organizational learning is candor and tolerance for conflict; cultures that tolerate and even encourage diverse opinions are generally far more successful than those that suppress disagreement.

After-Action Reviews should become a routine practice in every organization; make a habit of learning from your experiences. Embrace continuous improvement in the way you conduct meetings and welcome suggestions from all sources.

Looking Ahead

We've now covered all of the meeting "P's" except Place. In Chapter 5 we'll look at how the nature of a meeting's Place impacts the nature and tone of the conversation. I will also describe several specific examples of how a change of Place can produce a wholesale change in the ensuing conversations.

Chapter Five

FINDING "THE PLACE JUST RIGHT"

You understand instinctively that the place where a meeting occurs has an impact on the nature of the conversation. Just imagine the difference between a conversation around a large formal conference table with expensive executive chairs and one that takes place in an informal employee lounge, with the participants seated in a circle on soft bean-bag chairs.

Or consider the classic image of a boss seated behind a large desk, in front of a large window framing her silhouette as she delivers a performance review to a "lowly" subordinate sitting across the desk in a low, hard-back chair.

Now think about that same performance review being conducted on two softer wing chairs of equal height, with a low coffee table between them. Or in a nearby restaurant or coffee shop. Or on a trail in the woods adjacent to the corporate office. Which of those conversations do you think will evolve in a more caring, respectful, and supportive mode?

How Does Place Impact Process?

Every physical setting sends distinct signals to meeting participants—signals that set the tone and provide a context for the conversation, even when they are subtle or not in anyone's conscious awareness.

Here are brief descriptions of three very different settings for meetings. I am not suggesting that any one of them is "better" or "worse" in any absolute sense, but I want you to see that they represent three distinctly different contexts in which conversations can and do take place.

A formal executive conference room

The room is about forty feet long and twenty feet wide. One wall contains a long picture window; it provides a view from the building's twentieth floor of a city park with a busy superhighway beyond it. An extra row of chairs sits below the window. The opposite wall is covered with thick blue wallpaper; it holds three oil paintings hanging above a long credenza. On the credenza is a silver coffee set with china cups and saucers.

The dark walnut table that fills most of the room is oblong; it seats twelve people on a side. The accompanying executive chairs are on rollers, with padded leather seats and several height adjustment levers. At one end of the room is a white board with a retractable screen in the ceiling above it.

There is an LCD projector suspended from the ceiling; the audiovisual and lighting controls are behind an almost-invisible panel at the back of the room. In front of each chair is a leather executive writing pad. And arrayed down the center of the table is a row of electrical outlets and Internet ports.

Finally, adding another touch of formality, there is a microphone in front of each of those writing pads that connects to a telephone conferencing system; the speakers for remote participants who dial in to meetings are embedded in the ceiling.

Now, just imagine that you are a mid-level project manager who has been invited into this room to provide the executive committee with a progress report on your two-year, multi-million-dollar design project. What does it feel like? How open and candid do you expect the conversation to be? How warm and supportive will the committee members' questions feel?

A project team "war room"

Now imagine yourself back in the work room that your product design team has been using for the past eighteen months.

That room is about forty-by-forty feet; it has several smaller work tables scattered around the room, tables that can easily be moved together for whole-team meetings or separated for subgroup working sessions. The chairs are lightweight hard plastic with metal legs capped with smooth plastic buttons. The room has no windows; in fact, three walls have white boards while the fourth is half corkboard and half painted wallboard; all of them usually sport taped-up flip-chart paper filled with lists, project schedules, sketches, and some graffiti.

There is a large industrial clock on one wall, hanging just above a poster listing the company's latest vision and values statement. Along the rear wall there are three two-drawer filing cabinets; on one of them sits a coffee pot and a stack of paper cups, although most team members use the ceramic mugs that sport the project's logo which the team leader purchased six months ago to celebrate the team's first anniversary.

There are also two large plastic tubs along one side wall (one for trash, one for recycling bottles and cans). The trash basket is stuffed with several used pizza boxes that reflect a just-concluded working lunch. The room is typically filled with fifteen to twenty team members, sometimes convened in a single group meeting but more often working in smaller groups and constantly complaining about how loudly everyone else is talking.

Those conversations are almost always serious and task-oriented, although they also sometimes degenerate at the end of the day into gossip and sports-related banter.

The employee lounge and coffee bar

The employee lounge down the hall at the building's corner is a large, open, light and airy space. Along one wall is a long counter with cupboard space above and below and a stainless steel sink at one end. On the counter are several coffee makers—two for regular coffee, one for decaf. The upper cupboards contain coffee cups, bags of coffee grounds, boxes of tea, boxes of sugar, and containers of powdered non-dairy creamer. There is a large stainless steel industrial-looking refrigerator at one end of the counter.

About six feet in front of the long counter are several small round high-top tables, each surrounded by two or three bar stools. Beyond those tables along the opposite window wall is a row of three tables, each with three or four accompanying plastic chairs, and a banquette seat against the wall. The tables are off-white, with covered electrical outlets and Internet ports embedded in their centers; the banquette cushions are bright red. At one end of that row is a large, low, round coffee-table with several soft sofas arrayed around it.

Over the course of a day the company's employees come and go as they fill and refill their coffee mugs. At mid-day most of the tables (both high-tops and regular height) are filled with people eating their brown-bag lunches and chatting about their personal lives, their families, the local sports teams, and the weather.

But the rest of the day there are usually anywhere from one to three or four business-oriented meetings going on in the lounge area. Those meetings are deadly serious, but the conversations are often punctuated with laughter, heated debates, and lots of note-taking on both paper pads and laptops.

Place matters.

However, having choices about place matters even more.

While many of us who are knowledge workers move around frequently from one workplace to another, finding "the place just right" for getting a particular task done is often difficult. Sometimes we need a quiet place and sometimes we want to engage with colleagues informally, while at other times we attend meetings with either focused group decision-making or open-ended brainstorming agendas. Each of those activities works best in a different physical setting.

Okay, that makes sense. But how does the design of the workspace affect your mood, your creativity, your ability to concentrate? More importantly, how does place impact the nature and tone of your conversations? And how does a change of place change a conversation?

Change the Place, Change the Conversation

Several years ago one of my business friends inherited a staff of civil servants who were "retired on the job." They were disengaged, bored, putting in their time, and not particularly focused on performing. Gloria Young was at that time the Clerk of the Board of Supervisors of the City and County of San Francisco. That meant she was essentially the Chief of Staff for the Board; all the city employees supporting the Board reported to her.

Young developed a multi-faceted strategy for addressing her staff's malaise. She prepared formal, written job descriptions that included performance goals and metrics which she prepared collaboratively with the individual job holders, so the descriptions, goals, and metrics reflected their knowledge of their own responsibilities as well as hers.

Young also developed a "shadowing" activity that quickly became a cross-training and succession-planning program. Selected individual employees would spend a day or so a week actively observing, following, and "shadowing" one of their colleagues at work. This process not only helped the "shadower" learn a new job, but at the same time it helped the "shadowee" understand his or her job more completely.

Often during the shadowing process the shadower would stop the shadowee to ask a question like, "Why did you just do that?" or "Why are you filing that document in that drawer?" Those conversations not only helped the shadower understand what was happening, but they usually forced the shadowee to reflect on the work task, and the ensuing conversation often led either to deeper understanding of what needed to be done, or to a conscious redesign of the work.

These new conversations created a revolution within Young's team. Her staff learned to think much more actively about their own work as well as what their colleagues were doing. Details about work flows, procedures, and skill requirements were out in the open—there for all to see, to comment on, and to learn from.

But the most significant change that Young introduced—one that quite literally transformed the nature of the conversations in her department—was her purchase of a dozen inexpensive canvas folding chairs.

It had become obvious to Young that her team was mired in a set of routine habits that were relatively unproductive. Staff meetings were often uninteresting, low-energy, and full of issue avoidance. No one was engaged; the meetings felt like a waste of time, especially to her.

The staff meetings had traditionally taken place in the department conference room, which was a classic design: a big wooden table surrounded by uncomfortable chairs in a small, drab room with almost no natural light. There was a white board at one end of the room, and a projector for sharing presentation slides when needed. The side wall had a large but bland painting hanging over a credenza that could hold a pot of coffee and plastic cups, along with some extra pads of paper and a few nondescript ballpoint pens.

That set of blue canvas chairs led to a dramatic shift in the nature of the group's conversations.

When Young wanted to engage her staff in a brainstorming meeting, or one requiring a tough decision, she would tell everyone "It's time for a blue chair meeting." Each staff member would pick up a chair and the group would troop down to the building lobby, or outside onto the plaza (or somewhere else nearby) if the weather was nice.

The team would set up the chairs in a circle, sit down, and start talking to each other as if their ideas mattered (which of course they did). As Young told me, "The change in the setting, in combination with the informal chairs, created a completely new atmosphere that stimulated all kinds of creative conversation."

Apply this insight to your own experience. How different are the conversations that fill your conference rooms from the ones that take place in the employee lounge, in the company cafeteria, around the proverbial water cooler, or in a nearby restaurant over lunch or with an after-work adult beverage?

Place matters. Traditional conference rooms send all kind of signals about what kind of conversations are appropriate. That conference room I described earlier has a "head end" where the team leader usually sits—the position of power. And the formality of the table and chairs and white board or flip chart tells everyone what the meeting will be like and how it will unfold.

A few years ago SCAN Health Plan, based in Long Beach, California, undertook a major office renovation that was designed both to save space and money, but also to support a corporate initiative to break down silos and encourage much more active collaboration across teams.

Among the new design features were several public spaces that Diane Coles-Levine, the director of workplace solutions at SCAN at the time, called "collaboration parks." There is now one area on each floor that includes a glass-enclosed conference space filled with soft chairs, low tables, moveable writing tables, and lots of light and bright colors. No large, heavy conference tables!

And outside each of those "conversation pits" is an open area that typically includes three or four small, lightweight tables suitable for small group meetings. Each table has electrical and Ethernet ports built in, and a speaker phone to enable remote staff to participate easily in those meetings.

Finally, just beyond the open table area on each floor is a coffee bar accompanied by several small elevated tables that enable still more informal conversations.

Coles-Levine is convinced that those collaboration parks had a significant positive impact on the culture at SCAN Health, which in turn contributed to a measurable uptick in the organization's productivity and employee satisfaction.

I once consulted with a high-tech medical services company where the CEO believed fervently in the value of having the entire workforce in the corporate office every day. She was so convinced that face-to-face collaboration was critical that she actively discouraged her staff from working at home or other remote locations. In fact, because gasoline prices were almost $5 a gallon at that time, she was seriously considering subsidizing the cost of commuting from employees' homes to the corporate office to ensure that everyone came to the office every day.

However, in spite of her well-known opinions about working remotely, when we walked through the corporate office on one occasion we couldn't help but notice how many cubicles and conference rooms were vacant; we estimated that over half of the workstations in the building were empty that day.

Not only that, but later that afternoon several of us accidentally discovered that one of the company's most important product design teams was holding a one-week planning meeting at a nearby (but offsite) co-working facility. Our own team met at that same facility late one afternoon to debrief our work with the CEO, which is how we discovered the offsite product design team.

The product design team leader had opted to spend company money renting an open, informal conference room at the offsite location because he and his team wanted to get away from the stodgy (and relatively unused) corporate conference rooms and the inevitable interruptions to their intense conversations that would have occurred had they stayed onsite.

They changed their place to change their conversation. And it worked.

You Don't Need <u>A</u> Place to Work; You Need Place<u>S</u>

If you think about it for very long, you will realize that you don't need a workplace; you need workplaces.

Of course, you can only be in one place at a time. But whether you realize it or not, sometimes you need to be in one place, and sometimes in another.

As a knowledge worker, you use your head to create value. Sure, you use your hands too, but mostly just to hit some little square pieces of plastic in a particular sequence that produces images of text on an electronic screen. I'm sure that sometimes you use a pen to spread ribbons of ink on paper as another way to create and communicate your ideas. However, no matter how you record your ideas or other forms of communication, it's what goes on in your head that matters.

But here's what's important about Place and its impact on your corporate conversations: you use your brain in a lot of different ways, and I've learned over the years that where your brain is physically (and where it's been) has a lot to do with how well it produces what you want it to.

Sometimes you need to explore, to think, to create new ideas. Other times you need to express an existing idea, sharing it with your colleagues in a meaningful conversation.

When you are interacting directly with others in a phone call, a face-to-face meeting, or a working session, you are using not just your brain but your eyes, ears, and mouth (and sometimes even your nose) as well. That's how you translate what goes on in your head into meaningful words (and body language) that make sense to other people, and (hopefully) contribute to a group's creativity and innovation.

So what's the point? Isn't that all pretty obvious? In one sense, of course it is. But in another, I am not so sure that any of us fully understands or appreciates the impact that our physical surroundings have on either the quality or the quantity of the "stuff" that happens between our ears and comes out of our mouths.

I've been thinking about the impact of place on my work and my conversations because not too long ago I had the good fortune to spend almost three weeks in northern Italy accompanying my wife and a group of her fellow artists who were exploring the history, the art, and the architecture of that very special area. They did a marvelous job of capturing many of the incredible buildings, natural vistas, and people on paper and canvas.

The group was gracious enough to let me tag along, so I too became immersed in the ancient churches, museums, eleventh-century walled villages, monasteries, and wonderful country walking paths. The fresh air and light breezes during the day and the hearty food and rich conversations every evening (helped along in no small part by some of the best inexpensive red wine on the planet) refreshed my spirit in ways that I hadn't really known how badly were needed.

During that trip I experienced a personal renaissance of thought and energy that mirrors in a very small way the grand cultural Renaissance that took place in the hills of Italy over 500 years ago. Surely the sun, the hills, and even the majestic cathedrals of that far-away time had something to do with the burst of creativity that brought Western Europe out of the Dark Ages.

Now, my own artistic ability is limited to pointing a digital camera and clicking the shutter, but even that simple activity helped sharpen my sense of where I was, what colors, textures, and shapes were surrounding me, and how those signals were affecting my mood and our conversations.

My experience of getting away from "the office" and the simple space inside the four walls where I normally do all that head work awakened me to how profoundly our surroundings affect the way we think, what we think about, and what kinds of conversations we end up having.

Yet most knowledge workers spend almost all their work time in a fairly traditional office environment—four walls, a desk, some filing cabinets, and shelves full of books. Sure, there might be a family photo or two on the wall, and maybe a picture drawn by a child, but the fact is that no matter what you are trying to accomplish on a given day, the place where you are is almost always the same.

Yes, most of us usually hold team meetings in a conference room, although sometimes you may have a meaningful group conversation in a cafeteria or a coffee shop; but let's face it, most of the time you use the same place to read, write, analyze, list, sort, file, talk on the phone, and even meet with colleagues—at least when you are not on airplane or in some drab hotel room far from home.

What if you had lots of places to choose among, and could move from one to another as you move from one task to another? My instinct tells me you'd be a lot more creative in some kinds of places (rooms filled with art work, or with outdoor photos—or literally outdoor places?), more analytic in others (a library, or a bare-bones office?), and more thoughtful and reflective in yet another place (a church? a mountain retreat? a sailboat? a café?).

I am reminded of one corporate facility I toured recently. It was exceptionally impressive—open workspaces with low or no dividers, light and bright colors, lots of windows and natural light, and a wide variety of meeting rooms and open seating areas. I can't help but think I'd be creative and energized if I worked there regularly. The people who are fortunate enough to have access to that place seemed highly engaged with their work and with their colleagues.

But the deeper lesson for me was the incredible variety of spaces and places within that one facility. There were several different "zones" with different workstation layouts (some were traditional eight-by-eight square cubes, some used the increasingly popular 120-degree designs), but there were also several enclosed "personal harbors" for two-or-three-person meetings, private heads-down work, or phone conversations; a "kitchen" and café area with informal lounge furniture groupings; an outdoor patio area; and several more traditional conference rooms of varying sizes and designs.

I don't have detailed work behavior or productivity data from that particular workplace, but anecdotally it's clear that people are moving around frequently from one spot to another over the course of a day as individual and team activities change dynamically from one hour to the next.

I'm sure you get my point. When there are so many different kinds of knowledge work, why do we so often try to do it all in one kind of place? How much creativity and innovation have we lost forever by plopping people who do different kinds of work from day to day and even hour to hour into those all-too-common, drab, one-size-misfits-all cube farms?

Can't Think Straight? Take a Hike!

Sometimes it pays to get out of a place altogether. Here are a few more examples.

Diane Coles-Levine, who left SCAN Health in 2014 and is now the head of an independent consulting firm, is fond of saying, "It's a lot easier to think outside the box when you're not in one." That's her way of pointing out that cube farms are not the best environment for creativity and collaboration.

And as I have observed several times, when individuals make choices about where and when to get their work done they "own" those choices and are generally more committed to their work, more productive, and more engaged with their organizations.

About five years ago I was part of an international research project team that was seeking to define the attributes of an effective workplace. Our Swedish lead researcher asked each of us on the project team to take a photograph of our favorite part of our own office and then to post it on the project website.

What do you think those photos showed? Almost three quarters of us had independently taken a picture of the view outside the nearest window! We all valued our views of nature. My picture from my home office was of our backyard garden, and the view beyond of San Francisco Bay.

There is also solid evidence that hospital patients whose beds are next to a window with a natural view typically recover more quickly than those whose beds do not have views of nature. Roger Ulrich, the author of "View Through a Window May Influence Recovery from Surgery" (*Science*, 1984), described his research this way:

> Twenty-three surgical patients assigned to rooms with windows looking out on a natural scene had shorter postoperative hospital stays, received fewer negative evaluative comments in nurses' notes, and took fewer potent analgesics than twenty-three matched patients in similar rooms with windows facing a brick wall.

There's something about nature that we all find soothing, refreshing, and inspiring. Getting out of the box that is your office can have a powerful impact on your productivity, your emotional frame of mind, and even your sense of self-worth.

So when you are feeling stressed, or stuck, take a break; get up, get out of the office, and take a walk. Tony Schwartz and Christine Porath, in their May 2014 New York Times article "Why You Hate Work," tell a story about Luke Kissim, the CEO of Albemarle, a multi-billion dollar chemical company. Kissim realized he was personally burning out on the job, so he began taking a break at least every ninety minutes, and he often left the building to take a walk around the block.

Kissim then began insisting that all his employees follow suit. He's put over 1,000 of Albemarle's managers through a course that's teaching them how to invest in themselves and in their staff—and a big part of that investment is getting up and taking walks—outside the building.

Finally, another wonderful example of the value of getting back to nature is what's happened at Western Union's corporate headquarters in Englewood, Colorado. The company recently redesigned its facilities and landscaped the surrounding grounds to include walking/hiking trails through the woods.

I was fortunate to hear John Coons, Western Union's Vice President of Corporate Real Estate, talk about how many of the company's managers and staff are now taking regular outside walks (weather permitting, of course); and, more importantly, many of them have started holding critical one-on-one performance review conversations with their staff out on the trail.

Just think about how much more meaningful those conversations must be than if they were held in an enclosed office with a big desk separating the manager from his/her subordinate. As I have said so often, place matters. To change the conversation, change the place—and be sure to include Mother Nature in your definition of "place."

Pick the Place to Fit Your Purpose

So the next time you want a creative, high-energy meeting filled with open, authentic conversation, find a place that says "Talk openly, we're all in this together, let's have fun and get something done."

What does that kind of place look and feel like? When I want to encourage open, candid, and high-energy conversations, I look for physical settings that include:

- plenty of natural light

- bright but not overpowering colors

- simple artwork

- moveable tables and chairs (so the group can reconfigure the arrangement and take ownership of it)

- white boards and/or flip charts for note-taking

- simple refreshments (including fresh fruit and nuts, but not sugar-based products).

And if you can't do a wholesale office renovation to create those kinds of spaces, at least think about getting your own set of blue canvas chairs, or getting outside and away from the office.

As Gloria Young discovered with her blue chair meetings, a change of place can be refreshing and re-engaging even if you don't go off to a spa or a beach-side resort.

Even though a group meeting may be your best choice for addressing a particular issue, remember that you don't have to hold a traditional meeting in a traditional place (by that I mean one where you reserve a conference room, set a time, and convene the group around a conference table).

If your purpose is simply to make an announcement, or to provide a quick status report (perhaps you do that every Monday morning), consider a brief stand-up meeting in your office, or in a common area. That simple shift in both the Place and the Process can create an entirely different experience for the Participants, and usually produces a different kind of outcome as well.

Looking Ahead

Everything I've covered so far presumes that all the meeting Participants are in the same physical location. That is, the meeting is face-to-face, or in person.

What if the meeting participants are located in different places?

You know as well as I do that many (if not most) corporate meetings are now conducted by telephone or online. And those meetings are significantly different from traditional in-person meetings in more ways than you may realize. In Chapter 6 I'll share some observations about those differences and offer some more New Rules, this time for leading distributed conversations.

Chapter Six

WHAT IF EVERYONE IS SOMEWHERE ELSE?

Throughout this book I have been discussing conversations and formal meetings in organizational settings as if all them involved face-to-face or in-person communication. Yet you know from personal experience that many of your work-related conversations involve communicating with people who are somewhere else.

In fact, a full *two-thirds* of knowledge work today takes place outside of corporate facilities. That sounds like a strikingly large number, but I and many others have conducted numerous studies clearly demonstrating that organizational work is widely dispersed across many different kinds of locations. With modern technologies it doesn't seem to matter whether the people we are talking with are across a desk, across the room, across town, or on another continent.

Yet one of the most common complaints I hear about letting local employees work remotely even just a day or two a week is "How can I manage them if I can't see them?" Of course that attitude reflects many years of having immediate subordinates close by; most managers rely on "management by walking around" as a way to exercise control over their staff. The managers can see what their staff are doing, and they generally presume their physical presence acts a constant reminder of their authority and the need for everyone to stay busy.

Actually a more accurate way of understanding the reaction that many employees have to their managers constantly watching them (and even peering over their shoulders) is that they find all kinds of ways to *look* busy.

Workforce flexibility and mobility—whether it is called "telecommuting," "work from home," "flexible work," "remote work"" or something else—is rapidly becoming a way of life for more and more knowledge workers. As I have noted over and over again throughout this book, technology is increasingly able to connect people with each other, with information, and with work processes no matter where on earth they happen to be at any particular moment.

Many of us actually communicate with other people located somewhere else more often than we do with those who are sitting across the aisle or at the next workstation. For most of us telephone conversations and e-mail correspondence are the primary tools we use to interact with others today.

However, most people I know still prefer face-to-face conversations, especially when the subject is critical or emotional. And they believe that "F2F" communication is more effective than any other kind. Yet it is a fact of life that most of the work we do and many of the conversations we experience every day are distributed. And many of those "conversations" extend over time as well as over physical distance.

Managers often worry that distributed teams suffer from a loss of the serendipity that so often leads to important business breakthroughs—those unplanned, spontaneous conversations between people who don't interact normally in the course of doing their jobs, or who, when they do interact, are narrowly focused on the task at hand.

But even if we continue to prefer face-to-face meetings, the hard reality is that they are becoming a smaller and smaller percentage of our work experience. We all have to learn how to work effectively with people who are located in other places.

Yet in spite of that reality, most of us don't pay anywhere near enough attention to the many ways that those distributed conversations are different from in-person meetings.

In this chapter I want to review several often-unrecognized differences between in-person and distributed conversations. I will then suggest some guidelines and several more New Rules for making distributed meetings matter as much as their face-to-face counterparts do.

Background: The Exponential Growth in Distributed Conversations

One of my earliest studies of work patterns indicated that on average knowledge workers were spending only about 35 percent of their work time inside their assigned corporate facility. They were spending almost as much time working out of home offices, and the remainder in "Third Places" like coffee shops, libraries, public parks, hotels, airports, and planes, trains, and automobiles.

Today well over thirty million U.S. workers are spending one or more days a week in nontraditional work locations. That's over 26 percent of a nonfarm workforce that currently totals approximately 130 million. And it's worth pointing out that many agricultural workers are also highly dependent on mobile technologies, even if we don't normally think of them as part of the "remote" workforce.

Why is workforce mobility growing so rapidly and becoming the accepted way of working in so many industries? In my view it's not enough to point to the incredible explosion of personal, mobile computing devices (laptops, tablets, smartphones) and the infrastructure that supports them. WiFi has become nearly, if not totally, ubiquitous, and it is the price of being in business for most airports, hotels, and coffee shops, as well as public libraries, parks, and mass-transit systems.

But while the technology certainly *enables* workforce mobility, it is basic economics and employee preferences that are driving its explosive growth. Most people are thrilled to avoid those long commutes. One newly-remote worker told me, "I used to spend twenty dollars every couple of days on gas. Now it's more like twenty dollars every two weeks."

Another new remote worker told me that staying home several days a week had helped her lose ten pounds in just two months:

> Instead of sitting in my car on the freeway for an hour every morning, I take a thirty-minute walk before sitting down to work. And I'm eating healthy food from my own kitchen instead of running out to a fast-food place for lunch.

My research over the past ten years confirms that a flexible workplace strategy and an aggressive remote/distributed work program can reduce workforce support costs by 40 percent or more.

That is not an exaggeration. The biggest and most obvious source of those reductions is real estate and corporate facilities costs. Companies like Cisco Systems, Hewlett-Packard, Macquarie Bank, and Panduit Corporation, along with government agencies like the General Services Administration of the U.S. federal government, have reduced their investments in real estate and facilities by up to 50 percent, in some cases driving costs down by $50 million or more per year.

But there are other, more subtle workforce support cost-saving opportunities that go well beyond real estate and facilities. In almost every infrastructure area, from IT to HR to Administrative Support, remote/mobile workers generally operate more independently and need less support than do traditional office-based workers. In order to survive "in the field" remote workers have to learn to work on their own, and to solve their support problems quickly and inexpensively.

The bottom line on distributed work is that it reinforces the idea of treating employees like the responsible adults that most of them are. Remote employees quickly become self-managed employees. They take responsibility for their own work and the outcomes they produce.

I have seen data showing that remote employees are significantly more engaged with their company and its mission than their peers who are required to be in the corporate facility every day. That may seem counterintuitive, but when you think about it, the company is telling remote employees that it trusts them to make the right decisions about where, when, and how to get their work done. And they repay that trust with harder work, more emotional engagement, and a stronger commitment to their employer. Furthermore, most of them put in more effort because they don't want to lose the benefits of working from home.

Leading a Distributed Team

But my focus here is really not about the business case for distributed work. Rather, I want to offer some practical guidelines for team leaders who are responsible for distributed teams. Leadership in a distributed or flexible work environment is certainly more complex than it is when everyone is in the same physical location; but when done right it's actually easier and even more satisfying.

Start with the recognition that there are several substantive differences between the experience of being in an office every day, on the one hand, and working from home or some other remote location, on the other.

In some cases the team members live far away from each other and/or the central office. They may never have met in person, or they may see each other only occasionally. That's a very different kind of distributed work experience than one in which all the team members are based out of the same office but sometimes work remotely.

When team members are not co-located, they typically have relatively independent personal lives and social-support systems. Realistically, they just don't have a lot in common beyond their work. They go to different churches, synagogues, and mosques; they participate in different local town events; their children attend different schools and participate in different sports programs. And they just don't bump into each other at the grocery store or on commuter trains and buses.

In contrast, in a locally distributed team the members usually do know each other well, and they may often see each other outside the office—at local stores, schools, and community events. More importantly, they read the same newspapers and follow the same sports teams (although sometimes their children's teams are cross-town rivals).

Here is my first New Rule for leading virtual teams:

> In a widely distributed team the leader must spend significantly more time ensuring that team members get to know each other and share personal experiences.

In locally distributed teams that kind of personal catching up usually takes place for a few brief moments at the beginning of a conference call, or it happens more naturally when everyone is in the common office at the same time.

However, creating and leading a cohesive, smoothly running distributed team does require some special skills and approaches. Let's think first about the broader context in which distributed teams operate and then focus in on how to ensure that your conference calls and other forms of communication produce the kinds of outcomes you desire.

Context

To build effective distributed teams and ensure the context is right for meaningful conversation and productive work, leaders of distributed teams must master four basic but often unrecognized New Rules:

NEW RULE: Use highly participative approaches as you establish new distributed work environments. Pull out all your books and articles about introducing major organizational change, and follow their advice. Involving your team in defining the way it is going to work will instill a much higher level of commitment than if you simply impose mandates. It's another example of collaborative leadership being more effective than one-way command-and-control.

NEW RULE: Define and publish formal policies and procedures for distributed work. It's easy to slip into a potpourri of special arrangements for different individuals, but that's a recipe for disaster—if not lawsuits.

NEW RULE: Establish explicit, tangible performance measures. Managing a distributed workforce requires team leaders to shift their focus away from tight control of workers' activities and toward managing results or outcomes. It is critical that leaders and their subordinates agree in advance on how performance will be measured and rewarded.

The distributed work programs I have designed always include explicit processes for establishing performance "contracts" between participants and their managers. These contracts identify tangible results, specific deadlines, and other agreements about mutual accountabilities and support levels. And the good ones are tailored to each individual remote employee.

NEW RULE: Develop formal agreements about regular communication. A lack of direct and frequent communication often makes both managers and distributed workers uncomfortable. Periodic face-to-face conversations are important, but with effective telephone, e-mail, and instant messaging contact it doesn't have to happen as often as many managers might think. But some level of personal contact should occur at least once a week.

One of the most important aspects of managing a distributed team and keeping its members connected is understanding their work patterns and matching both technology-support and personal-management practices to their particular needs.

I have made extensive use over many years of a simple but powerful tool or framework for categorizing team activities that was first introduced by Bob Johansen and David Sibbet in their book *Leading Business Teams*. It basically sorts human interactions into four separate buckets:

- Same Time/Same Place

- Same Time/Different Place

- Different Time/Same Place

- Different Time/Different Place

The two dimensions of time and place combine to create a very useful model, as shown in Figure 6.1. This version includes several examples of technology tools that are appropriate for each kind of interaction.

FIGURE 6.1: Communication Across Time and Place

	Same	Different
Same	Conference rooms, flip charts, white boards	Audio, Video, and web conferencing
Different	Flip charts, Post-It notes, etc.	E-mail, blogs, wiki's social networking, collaborative workspaces

Time (vertical axis label, rows: Same / Different)

Place (horizontal axis label, columns: Same / Different)

The first thing you should do as a leader of a distributed team is assess the team's working patterns and determine what technologies it needs to get its core jobs done and to maximize the amount of meaningful communication among team members.

Interestingly, I have seen evidence in several of my clients that working remotely doesn't make team members lose touch with each other the way you might expect.

I was initially surprised to discover that when the members of a co-located departmental team at SCAN Health Plan were moved into a part-time work-at-home situation they actually reported feeling closer to their fellow employees than when they were all in the same building.

That's certainly counter-intuitive. But one team member described her experience this way:

> When we're all together in one place, I'm reluctant to interrupt anyone. They are all sitting in their cubicles with their backs to the door, their heads down, and they're often using headsets to speak with clients and other people by phone. But when we're all working from home, I have to pick up the phone to call them, or send an e-mail or instant message. It actually feels easier to connect with them now than it did before.

And I have seen a remarkably similar result, described in almost the same words, at National Equity Fund, a Chicago-based financial-services organization that supported its work-from-home program with several new technology investments. Instant messaging and more effective audio-conferencing tools made direct person-to-person communication far easier than it had been.

Leading Distributed Conversations

With all of this as background, here are several more New Rules for ensuring that your distributed meetings are both productive and personally engaging for the participants.

First, remember that the New Rules for leading in-person meetings that I identified in Chapters 3, 4, and 5 are just as important for distributed meetings.

Your basic challenge is to overcome the weaker relationships that widely distributed team members have with each other and the reality that the participants usually can't see each other, so there is almost no nonverbal communication (although videoconferencing from the desktop or laptop is getting close to broadcast quality, and is becoming more and more common).

And of course you also have the difficult challenge of keeping everyone engaged in the conversation in order to minimize multi-tasking—that horrible habit that almost all of us have of checking e-mails or working on unrelated tasks when we're participating in an audio conference call and no one else can see what we're doing.

Here are five specific rules a leader of a distributed meeting must follow to be effective:

- **NEW RULE: Publish an explicit agenda ahead of time**; encourage invitees to comment on or enhance the agenda in advance of the meeting and as you begin.

- **NEW RULE: Establish meeting "etiquette"**— guidelines for speaking, listening, debating, and so on; ask explicitly that everyone stay "tuned in" to the meeting and not attempt to multitask (e.g., checking e-mail, reading unrelated materials, etc.).

- **NEW RULE: Be sure everyone knows how to use whatever technology you are relying on**; schedule separate "training" sessions ahead of the meeting(s) if necessary; provide participants with a checklist for using the collaborative tools effectively; there is nothing more frustrating or more wasteful of participant time than having technology failures interfere with the flow of the meeting.

- **NEW RULE: Spend the first few minutes of each meeting "checking in" with the participants**; ask for personal news and updates as well as business-related activities.

- **NEW RULE: Respond to comments from others non-judgmentally**; listen carefully and look out for any emotional content; draw out the quiet members of the team; ensure that everyone has an opportunity to speak and express their ideas/opinions; but those five New Rules are just table stakes; to be truly effective, add these additional rules to your distributed team leadership manual:

NEW RULE: Be exceptionally clear about the team's mission, purpose, goals, and success measures. That kind of clarity helps keep the conversations on track and reduces the temptation to listen with only one ear because the topic seems irrelevant.

NEW RULE: Be certain that everyone on the team understands their particular roles and responsibilities— and everyone else's as well. That way whether you are reviewing project progress or brainstorming, participants are more likely to listen to each other and build on each other's ideas.

NEW RULE: Be far more explicit than usual about individual activities and experiences both inside and outside of work, as well as personal relationships and task interdependencies. Again, because team members spend so much less time in each other's presence, it is your task as team leader to be more proactive about bringing up these "invisible" elements that so often make or break a team.

When everyone is co-located there are many informal opportunities between group meetings to resolve issues, build common understanding, and just stay connected. When people are physically dispersed those opportunities are much harder to come by, and realistically they don't happen by themselves. Your responsibility as the team leader is to create conversations during team meetings that fill in that gap.

NEW RULE: Develop explicit communication protocols and etiquette guidelines—and define them collaboratively.

It's far easier to call someone out for speaking inappropriately or for being overly passive during your group calls if you and the whole team have actively discussed and agreed on how you will work together. Set up a regular, predictable meeting schedule, and then either work off a standard agenda or send one out in advance of each conference call.

And be explicit about conversational protocols as well. Agree on formal rules (or at least guidelines) for how long anyone will speak on each topic, how to respond to others, how to resolve conflicts, how to reach decisions. Focus on the same principles you know you have to follow for in-person meetings but that, again, are harder to enforce when people aren't looking each other in the eye.

After a distributed meeting you don't have the luxury of following up on tough issues "offline" during a walk down the hall back to your staff's individual workplaces. But don't forget that you can always pick up the phone for a private conversation after any group call, or in advance if you want to ensure that you and others are on the same page regarding controversial topics or particularly complex challenges.

It's also effective to precede each conference call with an e-mail that defines the meeting's goals and desired outcomes as well as an agenda. Then follow it up with a meeting summary or, if appropriate, a formal set of meeting minutes. These kinds of formal documents help to make the meeting more tangible, and they help everyone understand the outcomes of the meeting. There's no way to claim the conversation was ambiguous or unclear when you (or someone on the call) has produced a document that makes the outcomes and commitments to future action explicit.

And one final **NEW RULE:** if at all possible,

Do not schedule or permit what I call "mixed meetings."

That's a conversation that includes two or more people in the same place plus one or more others calling in from somewhere else. While sometimes it's necessary to do that because of individual schedules or the need to include someone with specialized expertise who is based somewhere else, I've almost never seen a mixed meeting go well.

It's far too easy for the people who are meeting together in person to forget about or ignore the remote participants. And for the remote participants the experience can be enormously frustrating. Most speaker phones prevent two people in different locations from being heard at the same time, so the technology just adds another barrier that makes a free-flowing exchange of ideas even more difficult than normal.

Even if the audio is unusually clear (and it often isn't) it can be difficult to follow the conversation or even to recognize who is speaking. And since most speaker phones prevent participants in one location from interrupting whoever is currently speaking, the remote attendees often feel like second-class citizens. And that leads them to tune out, start checking e-mail or working on something else, and generally disengage.

The only exceptions to that pattern of remote disengagement that I've seen were when the remote person was the focus of the meeting and was essentially lecturing to the in-person group.

The best way to make that kind of situation tolerable is to add video conferencing to the conversation. In my opinion mixed meetings that rely solely on audio simply aren't worth the effort.

As an outside consultant I was once asked to participate in a three-hour twenty-person meeting that was convened in a remote community by a foundation I was working with. It really did not make sense for the foundation to fly me half way across the country and put me in a hotel overnight so I could be physically present for that half-day meeting.

The first hour of the meeting went just the way I expected; it was hard for me to hear, and even harder for me to stay focused on the conversation. I couldn't tell who was speaking, and it was often difficult to understand what was being said.

Then during a short break one of the participants who was physically at the meeting connected with me using a screen-sharing application that included video. He and I spoke individually for a moment and then he turned his laptop around so his video camera faced the middle of the large round table in the center of the conference room.

Suddenly I felt part of the meeting; I could see most of the other participants, as well as their arm gestures and facial expressions. When one of them got up to write on a white board I could see the words and pictures she created. While it wasn't completely the same as being there, I found myself paying much closer attention, engaging with the conversation, and speaking much more frequently as well. For the remainder of the meeting I was a genuinely active participant.

That experience, more than any articles I've read or stories I've heard from other people, convinced me of the value of using video for distributed meetings. We are all accustomed to audio-only phone calls, and they seem perfectly sufficient for two-person conversations, especially when the two people know each other well. But video creates a far richer experience for group meetings than most of us realize. We don't understand what we're missing without it. In today's technology-rich environment that so often requires, and depends on, distributed meetings, there is a growing "toolkit" of hardware and software programs that can augment conversations among people who are widely distributed in both time and place.

There are many conference call platforms available in the marketplace today. Some are simply telephone systems—special numbers that everyone can call into. Many others are web-based; some are free (though the providers of those systems typically make their money off long-distance call charges that are often excessive).

The best conferencing systems include features that can sometimes make distributed meetings even more productive than face-to-face meetings. For example, most commercial audio systems enable you to punch in a code on your telephone that will automatically record the conversation, which can then be transcribed or at least made available to team members who could not participate in real time.

While the vast majority of distributed meetings are held using simple audio conference calling tools, video conferencing and screen sharing systems are becoming more common. As I noted above, full video increases attention dramatically, and of course it adds lots of nonverbal communication—posture, body language, and facial expressions—that enriches understanding and connections among meeting participants.

Let's briefly consider several specific examples of how these kinds of tools can augment a distributed meeting experience.

Cool Tool: Screen sharing tools enable the host or meeting leader to send a screen image of his or her computer monitor to all the other participants. That is of course the kind of technology that supports webinars in which one person "broadcasts" a web-based seminar or workshop to others (which can number from a few to a thousand or more listeners).

The most common use of screen sharing is to support a seminar or lecture. However, small teams can also share, review, and even co-edit a document that they are producing collaboratively.

There are also web-based platforms, usually called **interactive white boards**, that enable all participants to create free-hand drawings and/or text that can be seen by all the other participants in real time.

Finally, there are also **web-based document creation tools** that some distributed teams use to create online, real-time meeting minutes or notes that can be seen (and edited) by any of the participants who are signed on to the system during the meeting.

I've recently been part of a distributed team that relies on a web-based text platform called Hackpad (www.hackpad.com, another **Cool Tool**) as a means of documenting our conversations and developing (in real time during the meetings) formal statements for later publication or distribution to a larger group. With Hackpad all the meeting participants can not only contribute to those statements but they can also see them as they are being developed.

That particular tool has single-handedly helped that particular team converge quickly around a set of shared ideas and goals. It has also enabled people who miss a particular conversation to stay connected and to see firsthand the outcomes of meetings they were unable to attend. And it produces a far more engaging experience for all of us who are actively participating at the time.

Cool Tools for Measuring Meeting Behaviors

There is one more important category of meeting tools I want to mention. David Coleman, an expert and industry analyst focused on collaboration technologies, has recently noted that most meeting measurement systems focus on what he calls "meta-metrics"—how many meetings are held, how many people attend a given meeting, how long the meeting lasts—but there are almost no common metrics focused on behaviors in meetings, or on the content and outcomes of a meeting.

For example, Coleman asks how the quality of a meeting might be affected if there were real-time monitors that provide participants with feedback on what percentage of the time each person was speaking. That's not a difficult measurement task in a distributed meeting, where participants are connected by telephone or with an online conferencing system.

In Coleman's mind, that kind of information could have a constructive impact if, for example, everyone became aware that Phil was dominating the conversation and Susan had not said a word for over twenty minutes.

There are even technologies now available that can measure the emotional content of what people are saying, through voice recognition and tone-of-voice monitoring. For example, Humanyze (www.humanyze.com), a Silicon Valley firm launched by several alumni of the MIT Media Lab, has developed a "sociometric badge" that measures the frequency and duration of individual comments during both formal and informal meetings. The data the badge produces enable sophisticated analysis of social networks, individual contributions to group meetings, and even the intensity of the emotions being expressed. (The badge does not record actual content of the conversations, and is used only on an opt-in basis by individual employees).

While that kind of measurement might feel too much like "Big Brother" for many people, Coleman's ideas and the Humanyze badge do raise the intriguing possibility of how new technologies can enhance the quality of the meeting experience, and—presumably—the quality of meeting outcomes as well.

However, Coleman is quick to emphasize that in his experience (which is completely consistent with my own), the quality of a meeting depends far more on the skills of the meeting leader and, if present, a facilitator. That's true whether the meeting is in-person or distributed.

Finally, one other **Cool Tool** that is important for measuring meeting effectiveness is a post-meeting assessment. It might be overkill to conduct a formal assessment after every meeting, but a periodic feedback survey can be a very useful way to learn from the participants' experiences and focus your attention on meeting management issues that are concerning them.

Recall also the concept of the "After-Action Review" process that I described in Chapter 4. Gathering feedback, both objective and subjective, is an important practice for any kind of meeting, whether it's in a conference room or spread out over thousands of miles.

Looking Ahead

We are getting near the end of the book; we've covered both the Why's and the How-To's about making your corporate conversations more meaningful. I've urged you to be more intentional about all the conversations you engage in, both formal and informal. And we've looked at the impact that Purpose, Participants, Process, and Place can have on your meetings and their outcomes. We've just explored how to lead a virtual meeting in which the participants are physically separated.

It's relatively easy to pull a group of people into a conference room for a normal meeting or to take them to an offsite location for a more intensive strategic planning or problem-solving session. However, if you are attempting to address a really complex "wicked" problem and are looking for a major breakthrough experience you need to adopt radically different kinds of meeting methodologies—approaches that generate more candor, more creativity, and more commitment than normal.

And that's what the next chapter is about. It includes brief descriptions of six different approaches to designing and conducting organizational meetings that are capable of producing extraordinary outcomes. Whether it's resolving a decades-old conflict, redesigning basic business processes, producing radical new product designs, or reinventing the organization from the ground up, one of the approaches described in Chapter 7 might be just what you need to produce a true transformation.

Chapter Seven

DESIGNING AND LEADING EXTRAORDINARY MEETINGS

M ost of this book is focused on how to lead meetings that matter under normal conditions and in the course of day-to-day work. However, there are also many special-purpose meetings that require different kinds of leadership, different agendas, and different conversation processes. This chapter explores several powerful and well-tested meeting methodologies that can enable you to produce impactful outcomes in a relatively short time.

This is by no means a comprehensive catalog of meeting methodologies; rather I have chosen a half-dozen approaches that I am either personally familiar with or I have learned to appreciate because of personal conversations with experienced experts and practitioners.

Before we dig into those special ways to design corporate conversations with impact, let's take just a few moments to think more broadly about corporate meetings and the challenges you face as a meeting designer and leader.

Change the Outcome by Changing the Process

This book has described New Rules and a few cool tools for what I call "traditional" corporate meetings—activities involving a group of people having a relatively structured conversation about a work-related issue or opportunity.

I've also pointed out how the ways in which a meeting is structured, and where it's located, can impact both the conversation process and its outcomes. But I haven't pushed those boundaries very far.

There are actually many other ways to set up, structure, and lead meetings—meeting design approaches that provide unusual opportunities for the participants to express themselves and— even more importantly—to generate creative ideas that can address serious issues more effectively, and more efficiently, than traditional approaches.

I am excited about these "alternative" meeting design methodologies because each of them offers a powerful, well-tested way to transform a collection of individual experiences and ideas into a collective solution for gnarly, wicked problems. They are wonderful examples of the adage I've repeated so often throughout this book: under the right conditions, all of us together are far smarter and more powerful than any one of us individually.

There are six different special approaches described here:

- **Scenario Planning**, a particularly effective form of creating visions of the future in the face of dynamic uncertainty.

- **Future Search**, a comprehensive approach to developing a strategic vision and building both consensus and commitment to make the vision a reality.

- **The World Café**, an effective way to engage large numbers of people in conversations of discovery and creativity.

- **Business Process Redesign**, an analytic process that focuses on reinventing core operational practices.

- **Work-Thrus**, a variation on the General Electric "workout" process that, again, engages a large number of people in addressing and resolving "wicked problems" in a short period of time.

- **Organizational Jams**, organization-wide conversations that draw on the talents and experiences of literally thousands of people through the use of online networks and special-purpose software.

In every case there are original source materials that go into much greater depth that I have space for here. I've listed the most important books and websites in the Resources and Notes section at the end of the book.

Scenario Planning

Historically, strategic planning was all about focusing an organization's attention on a particular marketplace and ensuring that it had the operational capabilities to compete effectively in that market segment. Most strategic plans make explicit assumptions about future trends and probabilities, and they usually include educated guesses and formal statistical projections about what the planners expect will happen. However, in today's highly volatile and unpredictable world, assuming any kind of predictability in the marketplace can be fatal.

Traditional strategic planning is worse than useless when dealing with the uncertainties of today's economy. Indeed, traditional thinking about the future, as if it were actually singular and knowable, is downright dangerous.

The best way I know to embrace uncertainty and engage in constructive, collaborative speculation about the future is called scenario planning.

Scenarios are stories about the future that, when taken together, describe a range of plausible future states of an industry, its markets, and a particular business. Scenarios are a tool for dealing with rapid change, uncertainty, and inherent unpredictability. Scenarios are not predictions of the future; rather, they are images of *possible* futures, taken from the perspective of the present.

Because scenarios are developed explicitly to describe a range of possibilities, they help organizational leaders open their minds to the inherent uncertainties in the future, and enable them to consider a number of alternative "what-if" possibilities without immediately needing to choose or commit exclusively to any one most-likely outcome. Scenario analysis enables managers, business planners, and executive teams to develop multiple options for action that can be compared and assessed in advance of the need to implement them.

An effective scenario suggests critical implications for the organization and contains personal meaning for the people who build it. Scenarios are useful tools primarily because they facilitate—indeed, *require*—a strategic conversation about the unpredictable outcomes of today's rapidly changing business environment.

While there are many different approaches to developing scenarios, my personal preference is to follow a three-stage process:

> First, begin by identifying the most critical and potentially impactful unknowns—the things you realize you don't know today that if you did know would tell you how to make effective decisions today about tomorrow.
>
> Second, select two of the most critical of those unknowns—two uncertainties that are essentially independent variables. Each of these two dimensions of

the future should have two equally likely but unpredictable outcomes (as far as you can tell at this point; if the opposite outcomes are not equally likely, the variable isn't really an uncertainty).

Third, once you've identified those two critical uncertainties, set up a two-by-two matrix and look at the four possible combinations. Name them, and flesh them out to create four compelling stories that capture four alternative visions of the future.

Developing the actual scenarios into full-blown stories requires a group to abandon their basic assumptions about the future and to engage in imaginative brainstorming. That's not always easy for pragmatic executives to do, but playing "what if" games can be highly engaging and even fun.

Once a set of scenarios has been developed, a meaningful strategic conversation can begin in earnest. Which future scenario is closest to where we are today? Which one will unfold in reality if the key scenario drivers—business trends, regulatory policies, technological innovation—continue their present course? Which "world" would we prefer to be in? Is there anything the organization could do to actually "nudge" the future in one direction or another? What new kinds of competitors could emerge in each scenario?

Those kinds of questions, and the conversations surrounding them, inevitably create a sense of confidence about the future. Even if the scenarios are challenging or require dramatic change in strategic direction, regaining a sense of what can or could be done to thrive in that future is incredibly energizing.

Just as importantly, the identification of the key uncertainties that produced the scenarios increases the participants' awareness of what could happen. That sensitivity focuses attention on the critical variables that will eventually determine which scenarios are becoming more and more likely, and enables an organization to take appropriate anticipatory action to leverage opportunities or prepare for future challenges.

Future Search

How many times have you completed a strategic planning exercise, or a visioning effort, with high energy, high hopes, and exuberant optimism that the effort will finally—finally!—produce meaningful change, only to see everything evaporate in the face of organizational resistance and/or apathy?

Achieving lasting and meaningful change in large organizations often feels impossible. It's like Sisyphus rolling that boulder up the mountain, only to see it cascading back down to the valley, and having to start pushing it uphill all over again—and again, and again.

A Future Search Conference is a highly effective technique for getting that boulder to stay at the top of the mountain.

The approach was invented/developed by Marvin Weisbord and several colleagues in the early 1990s. It is documented, with plenty of tips and techniques along with several very compelling case examples, in *Future Search: Getting the Whole System in the Room for Vision, Commitment, and Action*, by Weisbord and Sandra Janoff.

The basic concept of future search is embedded in the book's subtitle. It involves bringing all the stakeholders in an organization together for a structured conversation that includes confronting issues candidly, surfacing differing perspectives and visions, building a common vision of a desirable future, and then developing a workable plan for achieving that vision.

Future Search works for several reasons, not the least of which is the presumption that every stakeholder brings legitimate experiences and expectations to the conversation. Future Search facilitators must be skilled at both sticking to an agenda and enabling differences in perspective to surface, be heard, and be accepted. It's not an easy task!

Future Search conferences are built on four basic principles:

- Get all the stakeholders in the same room (engage the whole system).

- Explore the whole "elephant" before trying to fix any part.

- Focus on the future and on common ground, not on problems or conflicts.

- Encourage self-management and personal responsibility for actions and results.

1. Engage the Whole System

It is exceedingly rare for all the stakeholders in any situation, with all their knowledge, experience, and perspectives, to be actively involved in problem-solving at the same time. As a result many organizational problems and inefficiencies persist for years because there's always some point of view or understanding that was left out—and thus there are "outside" critics who resist proposed improvements because their perspectives weren't included in the solution design process.

Involving all the stakeholders usually means that there will be people in the room from many different functional groups and, more importantly, from different levels in the organization (even from different organizations).

As the late New York Senator Patrick Moynihan once said, "Everyone is entitled to their own opinions, but not their own facts." The first phase of a Future Search conference is to get all the facts (and opinions) out in the open so everyone can see the "whole elephant." And that is precisely what principle number two demands.

2. Explore the whole elephant before trying to fix any one part

Constructive conversations begin by identifying areas of agreement rather than differences. If there is too much conflict or disagreement early on it can become incredibly difficult to build up any interest in finding common ground or even agreeing on common goals.

So the early focus of a Future Search conversation is on reaching a common or shared understanding of the "whole elephant"—the broad issue or challenge the group is facing. It's worth staying at the hundred-thousand-foot level initially in order to create that common view of what the group is facing and where it wants to go as a group.

And the experience of creating a common understanding of both history ("How we got here") and causality ("Why things are the way they are") helps the future search participants develop into a single community with a shared understanding of the past and present—necessary precursors to designing a shared future vision.

3. Focus on the future and common ground, not on problems or conflicts

Principle Three highlights the importance of finding common ground before getting caught up with differing views and values. Focus on the "big picture" and find views that everyone can agree with; that makes it much easier to confront differences, or to hone in on particular topics that may not even be of interest to everyone.

The primary objective of Future Search facilitators is to get the group focused on the future; because the future doesn't yet exist, broadly stated visions of where the group can go, or wants to go, can also serve to unite the participants and build emotional energy for moving forward and taking actions that will make a desirable future more likely to actually happen.

4. Encourage self-management and personal responsibility for actions and results

Most of the conversations during a Future Search conference take place in small groups—no more than three-to-five people around a table. Usually all the small groups are addressing the same questions or carrying out the same assigned tasks.

However, it is critical for the participants in those groups to be free to manage their conversations on their own. If the facilitators impose too many "rules" or restrictions on the small group conversations, the participants may feel constrained in what they can say, and they will certainly not feel adequate responsibility for the outcomes of their conversations.

Self-management empowers first the small groups and then the group as a whole to share leadership, to develop and enforce norms for acceptable behaviors, to document and report on their own ideas and decisions, and to ensure that everyone in the group has been heard and is valued for their contributions.

The World Café©

Imagine a room full of people talking animatedly with each other in small groups; everyone is talking about the same question. After twenty minutes the conference host, standing in the center of the room, raises her hand and waits until the room quiets down as more and more participants notice her and honor her non-verbal request for silence.

Once the group is quiet and totally focused on the host, she announces, "It's time to switch tables. I want one person at each table to stay where you are so you can be the historian of the ideas you've talked about so far. The other three of you get up and move to three other tables. Then, once everyone is seated again, continue your conversation about the same question."

Then, after another twenty minutes the host repeats the same intervention once again. Participants move to yet another table and continue the conversation again, with three new partners. The distinctive genius of the World Café approach is that it provides participants with multiple opportunities to address the same question in conversations with different people.

That simple concept guarantees an enormous amount of diversity in ideas and insights, lots of creative thinking, and high levels of energy and engagement. And it works well for any group of people, whether they know each other in advance or not.

The World Café model stems from a very simple, but incredibly profound, recognition: when (for example) one hundred people of almost any age over twenty convene for a meeting there is probably well over one thousand years of experience in the room. What a shame—and a lost opportunity—it would be to confine ninety-nine of those people to "listen-only" mode and in effect deny that their experiences and ideas have any value.

In contrast, a World Café creates a "collective intelligence" by unleashing the combined experiences and insights of all the participants.

Yes, there are experts who have something well worth listening to, and sometimes we just want to listen and learn. But, as Steven Campbell, author of *Making Your Mind Magnificent* (Aviva Publishing, Lake Placid, New York, 2010) has pointed out so eloquently, adults learn by linking new information and ideas with their existing neural networks of experiences, emotions, and knowledge.

However, that linking takes time; we need to ponder what we've just heard, relate it to our past experiences, and make sense out of it. That's hard to do when we are in listen-only mode, even though most of us can think about seven times faster than we can listen.

That is why experienced World Café leaders advocate at least twenty minutes per conversational round, three twenty-minute rounds on each important question, and a maximum of four people at each table. When the groups are larger or the time per round is shorter the conversations do not generate enough breadth and depth to produce meaningful learning. The most effective World Café's last a minimum of two and a half hours, and often extend over several days.

It is also worth noting that the World Café model is almost infinitely scalable. You can include as many four-person groups as you want to. World Café's have been conducted successfully in conjunction with major events involving as many as three to four thousand people.

Think for a moment about the most important questions you would like to explore in conversation with colleagues, either professionally or personally. There are seven core design principles you would want to rely on to ensure a successful World Café:

1. Set the context

2. Create hospitable space

3. Explore questions that matter

4. Encourage everyone's contribution

5. Cross-pollinate and connect diverse perspectives

6. Listen together for patterns, insights, and deeper questions

7. Harvest and share collective discoveries

For more information about those principles and how to apply them, pick up a copy of *The World Café: Shaping Our Futures Through Conversations that Matter*, by Juanita Brown with David Isaacs and the World Café Community.

Let me demonstrate how those principles affect the conversational experience with a story about a successful World Café I helped organize and lead.

Several years ago my then-business partner Charlie Grantham and I hosted a two-day extended conversation about the future of work—we rather boldly called it "The First World Congress on the Future of Work".

We were very fortunate to have the event hosted by our friend Gloria Young at San Francisco's magnificent City Hall. She was at that time the Clerk of the Board of Supervisors of the City and County of San Francisco, meaning she managed all of the administrative staff supporting the Board and the individual Supervisors. Young was the inventor of the "blue chair" meetings described in Chapter 5.

Our World Café/World Congress was held over two days in the magnificent South Light Court just off the Rotunda on the main floor of San Francisco's Civic Center.

In the interest of fostering wide-ranging conversations about the future of work and enabling the participants to get to know each other at a deep level, we declared the World Congress to be a "PowerPoint-free zone" and planned an agenda that included no formal presentations of any kind and only a very few platform speakers.

The participants were seated at small four-person tables (generously lent to us for the event by Herman Miller, which also supplied the Aeron chairs that surrounded each small table).

All the platform presentations together covered only four distinct topics:

1. Welcoming the attendees as the Congress opened;

2. Describing (very briefly) the discussion questions we wanted everyone to explore at their tables;

3. Offering guidelines to ensure that the "table talk" was meaningful; and

4. Letting everyone know when the breaks would take place, where the restrooms were, and what time we would adjourn for the day.

The entire event felt like a large, high-energy coffee house; we led the delegates in a series of brief but focused conversations on several very important questions about the future of work.

Now, if that was all there was to the World Café it might be a fun and energizing experience, but all the wonderful ideas that emerged would be lost. So with David Isaac's guidance we took several steps to capture the ideas, stories, and concepts that emerged from those conversations:

■ We provided each table with butcher paper and marker pens, and encouraged everyone to write down key ideas and to sketch out pictures that captured those ideas. Adults like to sketch and draw pictures as much as children in a restaurant do; visual thinking opens up much more of the brain than simple reliance on spoken words. The pictures the participants drew not only enriched the conversations in real time, but they created a historical record that we could review and extract from as we prepared meeting summaries.

- We also brought in a professional graphic recorder who created visual story boards of the summaries and report-outs that we asked each table to share with the group at large at the end of each day. Just like the individual doodling at the small tables, the graphic record of the whole-group conversation enriched everyone's understanding and provided vivid images that created long-lasting memories of the experience.

- We also took a number of informal photographs and several live video recordings of a few of the conversations (those images were intended more to showcase and promote the World Congress after the fact than to provide a documentary record, but they did provide some additional insights into the experiences of the participants—particularly their emotions and energy levels around certain issues).

About two weeks after the World Congress I spoke with one of the participants, a senior architect with a large federal government agency. When I asked him how he liked the event he responded enthusiastically that he had never before had an experience anything like it. He commented, "I have business cards from about twenty people who I know I can call up with any question and they'll get back to me right away. I've been to hundreds of conferences and that's never happened before."

I hope you recognize that those seven World Café design principles I listed earlier are applicable for any conversation you lead or participate in; they are by no means unique to the World Café model.

Business Process Redesign

One of the great examples of changing corporate conversations was the tsunami of business process-reengineering projects that swept through corporate America (and beyond) in the late 1990s.

Driven by the explosion of new technology capabilities and new kinds of information systems and databases, business process reengineering, or BPR, had all the hallmarks of a management revolution.

Unfortunately, like so many other organizational "revolutions," BPR bumped up against established management practices and cultures. Too many senior executives, lacking both imagination and courage, saw BPR as a way to squeeze their organizations into doing more with less. Regrettably, BPR became just another name for cost reduction and layoffs.

However, its core principles were, and still are, solid, and its potential for dramatically improving business operations and outcomes is truly impressive. Even though the approach is now over fifteen years old, its lessons and principles remain valid and valuable today.

Here's a brief recounting of a reengineering project that I played a key role in.

Imagine for a moment that you are the Chief Information Officer of a very large, 140-year-old life insurance company. Because insurance is fundamentally an information processing business, you are at the very center of your company's operations.

Your CEO has recently announced a major organizational change initiative to revitalize the company's culture, refresh its mission and values, and improve its bottom line. You are supportive of those goals but unsure how you and your staff of software and hardware engineers can contribute.

Your technology platform (based on mainframe computer architecture) is solid and your systems are running smoothly. You don't see much room for efficiency improvement, and you don't want to weaken your group's core values that emphasize stable, reliable operating systems, explicit quality control procedures, and predictable software development practices.

However, you are concerned that the company's independent life insurance agents, who are the lifeblood of the business, are increasingly frustrated with the cumbersome nature of the policy application and approval process.

On average it takes the company thirty to forty days to process and approve a new policy application. And your agents report that often when they take the approved policies back to their customers, they discover that the customers have changed their minds or decided to purchase a policy offered by a competitor.

Fred Albertson (not his real name), the CIO, became convinced there was an opportunity for dramatic performance improvement. He convened a small project team—initially from within his own IT department—to begin exploring the possibilities and building a business case.

The team first looked seriously at how several specific new technologies might enable them to process the policy applications more efficiently. Since they were all IT professionals, it was a natural starting point for their investigation.

However, even their most ambitious estimates suggested that at best they might be able to shrink the application approval process by about 15 percent, or four-to-five days. That clearly wasn't going to raise the customer conversion rate high enough to create a positive ROI for the cost of acquiring and installing the new technology.

At that point Albertson became aware of an article in the *Harvard Business Review* that was creating a serious buzz among his fellow

IT professionals. The author was MIT professor Michael Hammer and the article was titled: "Reengineering Work: Don't Automate; Obliterate" (July-August, 1990).

Hammer's basic thesis, and deliberately radical idea, was that using IT to automate an existing business process was the equivalent of pouring concrete over a company's information flows, locking them in place forever.

Hammer's call for obliteration rather than automation grew out of a very different mindset: start with the technology that is currently available and design a brand-new business process around that technology. Throw out, or obliterate, the old ways of doing things; start over; and take advantage of what modern technology enables you to do.

In Albertson's case this approach meant starting with the interaction between the life insurance agent and a prospective customer, and imagining how they could complete the application online from the very beginning. It actually took very little imagination to design a theoretical application and approval process that could be completed in less than three days (in contrast to the existing thirty-day process).

But imagining such a radical redesign and actually implementing it in Albertson's company was a lengthy and complex process— one that involved significant interdepartmental conflict, long team meetings, and plenty of heated conversations.

Those activities played out over a year-long redesign project. Once he obtained approval from the executive committee to launch the redesign project Albertson assembled a core team of senior directors and managers from IT, Customer Service, Marketing, Sales, and Accounting. That core group was supplemented and supported by a small team of outside consultants (including me) who brought expertise in both the insurance industry and business process reengineering.

The team then developed a charter and work plan that included five basic principles:

- Document the existing process to understand all the activities, information flows, decisions, time cycles, and costs in detail.

- Start with a clean sheet of paper and build an ideal process, leveraging modern technology wherever possible.

- Take nothing for granted, and challenge every assumption.

- Flesh out the new process design, and build a prototype using real technology and real people to make sure that what works in theory will work in practice.

- Build a business case, but only after proving that the new design would meet previously defined performance goals.

The project team's meetings stretched out over several months, and often lasted until eight or even nine in the evening.

What kept those meetings going? In hindsight, there were several factors that combined to make the team's conversations truly extraordinary:

- There was a strong, shared sense of both urgency and importance; the team members knew the current process was broken and that it was not producing the business results the company needed.

- The project had the blessing and sponsorship of the company's Chairman and CEO. It was both high-stakes and high-visibility.

- The project had also been positioned as a prime example of the Chairman's new culture change initiative that emphasized high standards and shared responsibility for success.

- The team members knew they were among the company's high performers and fast-trackers; being part of the project was viewed as a career-enhancing opportunity.

- The long afternoon/late evening meetings often included pizza and soft drinks as a way to keep the work going—but the meals also led to plenty of social conversations and much laughter. The team members got to know each other far more intimately than was typical in the organization.

- The opportunity to produce such a radical shift in the way policies were sold and approved was exciting, energizing, and meaningful.

So a project that began as a technology upgrade ended up transforming almost the entire company. Here are some of the performance outcomes the team's conversations produced:

- The policy application and approval process was shortened from an average of thirty-two days to less than four days.

- In the first year after the new process was implemented the company realized a significant increase in new policy sales.

- That increase in turn reduced the first-year attrition rate of new insurance salesmen from well over 50 percent to less than 25 percent.

- The redesigned customer service center not only cut its administrative costs dramatically, but it also increased customer satisfaction.

- The customer service group transformed from being a dead-end job with high attrition rates to a source of new insurance agents. What had been seen as a clerical job with little or no growth potential became instead a "farm team" where ambitious younger employees could learn about the company's products and competitive offerings before applying to become indepentent insurance agents.

The major reason those outcomes were so impressive is that the BPR project team began with a "clean slate."

The team was operating under unusual conditions that generated "out of the box" thinking, extraordinarily imaginative and candid conversations, and a strong commitment to producing meaningful results.

Work-Thrus

Now imagine this: you are in charge of integrating the activities of thirty-nine separate Blue-Cross/Blue Shield organizations, each with its own history, its own management structure, and its own carefully developed business processes for handling claims, supporting policyholders, and collecting payments.

Yet those thirty-nine separate businesses are all serving a common customer base: federal employees.

That is not a hypothetical situation; in fact, it is precisely where Rod Collins found himself when he became the Chief Operating Executive of the Blue Cross Blue Shield Federal Employee Program (FEP), a business alliance comprised of those thirty-nine separate organizations.

Collins describes his efforts to seamlessly consolidate the operations of thirty-nine independent companies in his impressive book *Leadership in a Wiki World*. He particularly highlights the sequence of structured activities that he developed to build consensus and shared understanding/commitment across those thirty-nine separate groups.

When Collins took over the FEP organization those thirty-nine businesses were in constant conflict and debate about how to become more efficient and more customer-focused.

He reflected at one point that ". . . we needed to improve the effectiveness of our meetings and the quality of our corporate conversations."

And he told me privately,

> "I was highly motivated to change the way FEP designed its work flows and chose how to get things done. I had inherited thirty-nine independent Blue Cross Blue Shield organizations, each one convinced its way was the best way. Every time we tried to define a new procedure or improve our efficiencies, we found ourselves in the middle of an intense, winner-take-all debate. However, there were no winners because we could never reach real closure. Thus, the debates were never-ending.
>
> We had to do something to stop those debates; it had become completely politicized."

The "Work-Thru" process that Collins developed over several years, with lots of experimentation, was designed to produce consensus about the best way to carry out a particular FEP business process or resolve a specific organizational issue that was getting in the way.

The Work-Thru process goes like this:

Pre-Meeting. Each Work-Thru effort is scheduled at an offsite location, for two or three days. All stakeholders who have relevant information or will be impacted by the process under review (usually forty to fifty people) are invited to participate.

The issue is defined briefly in the invitation, and an expectation is set that the Work-Thru will produce consensus and recommendations for action.

In most cases it was also clear that the group was not authorized to make a final decision or to commit resources to implement any recommended changes. A Work-Thru produces recommendations, group consensus, and a clear readiness to implement, but the formal commitment to proceed remained an executive-level responsibility.

Stage One: Presentation(s). Everyone arrives at the meeting site, and is encouraged to sit wherever they wish. Most participants end up sitting with friends and colleagues.

The Work-Thru host makes a very brief introduction to the meeting, restating broad goals but not addressing the focal issues. The person who has the most knowledge of the issue being worked through then delivers a twenty-minute presentation describing the issue and highlighting the challenges as he or she sees them (in some cases there could be more than one opening presentation).

During this opening presentation there are absolutely no interruptions allowed. The attendees are essentially in listen-only mode; the goal of Stage One is to gain understanding of the starting position, not to challenge it, reject it, change it, or adopt it.

Stage Two: Clarifying Questions. Immediately after the opening presentation(s) everyone is invited to ask clarifying questions. The important principle operating at this stage is that no one is allowed to offer an opinion, a judgment, or any suggestions for enhancements to the presenter's ideas. No criticisms; the only purpose of Stage Two is to enable the group as a whole to gain a deeper and more complete understanding of the presenter's perspectives and/or recommendations.

Stage Three: Small Group Discussions. At this point the larger group is split into discussion groups of eight-to-ten participants, each at a separate table. Each group's primary task is to identify and agree on the three-to-five most important observations, opinions, or concerns that group members share about the proposal or the challenge that has been presented.

However, before those small group discussions begin, the facilitator "remixes" the groups to ensure that most participants are not sitting with their bosses or others from the same functional team. In Collins' view this is one of the most critical design components of the entire experience. "We have to be certain that everyone feels free to express themselves without any fear of repercussion, and without stifling themselves because of pre-existing relationships."

Stage Four: Large Group Discussion. Then, finally, the group reconvenes as one body. First the small groups each report out their three-to-five key questions or insights. At this point the host/facilitator leads a single conversation that includes all the participants. Now, at last, is the time when opinions can be freely expressed.

Note that the conversation now focuses on the ideas, questions, concerns, and (eventually) on the group's solution recommendations, not on who first raised an issue or proposed a solution. This separation of ideas from individuals is another critical design factor that Collins is convinced helps to produce high-quality recommendations and widely shared understanding and commitment.

The most critical factors in this process are, of course, the strength and skills of the group facilitator (who, according to Rod Collins, should be the senior-most executive in the room). However the facilitator's commitment must be to the Work-Thru process, not to the content or outcome of the conversations. Those are the group's responsibility; the leader/facilitator's role is to implement the process fairly and effectively, and to strive for group consensus, independently of where the group wants to go.

It is clear to me that if people believe their ideas, suggestions, and requests have been listened to in a thoughtful, noncritical way, they will usually accept a decision or an action even when they don't completely agree with it. More than anything else, they want to be heard; and while they would like their ideas to "win," they will generally go along with decisions they don't like if they truly believe they have been treated with respect and listened to.

And that's why the Work-Thru process is so important, and so central to Collins' success.

Organizational Jams

How can you get everyone in on the action, and still get action?

One of the biggest challenges for many large organizations is creating opportunities for ideas about new products or process improvements to get adequate levels of attention.

Some organizations have set up internal "venture capital" groups that operate just like independent VC firms; they accept proposals for new businesses or new products and review them just like those independent venture capitalists. They select promising ideas, listen to the inventor pitches, and offer seed funding for the ideas they believe are promising and have the potential for eventually generating meaningful revenues.

Other firms—most famously 3M, but also including Google and other high-tech organizations—actively encourage their employees to spend a specified amount of work time (typically 10 to 20 percent, or a half-day to a full day per week) on creative projects that are unrelated to their current job responsibilities.

And still other organizations have experimented with various kinds of "jam sessions"—intense, open meetings or workshops where large groups of employees (and sometimes non-employee volunteers as well) come together for a day or more to tackle a "wicked problem." The goal is not just to brainstorm ideas but to actually produce solutions.

What is an Organizational Jam?

These kinds of meetings are often called "organizational jams" or "jam sessions" in the spirit of jazz musicians who gather in a club somewhere, invite anyone with an instrument to join them, and play spontaneous improvised music that is the sum total of all the individual contributors' creativity.

Some large organizations have employed digital technologies to create internal idea marketplaces that enable *anyone* in the organization to express their ideas and/or opinions independently of the formal reporting structures.

An organizational jam is essentially a very large-scale online collaborative conversation—a conversation in the same sense that Facebook posts and Twitter exchanges and e-mail threads are conversations. A jam is an opportunity for hundreds and even thousands of people to weigh in on a common problem or challenge; it's essentially the digital equivalent of a public forum, a Facebook stream of comments, or a LinkedIn threaded discussion—but on a much larger scale.

One of the first massive organizational jams I know of was a "Values-Jam" organized and conducted by IBM in 2003. Its intent was to enable as many of IBM's employees as possible around the world to contribute to the company's first re-examination of its core values in one hundred years.

The company describes the 2003 Values-Jam this way:

> Through "Values-Jam," an unprecedented seventy-two-hour discussion on IBM's global intranet, IBMers came together to define the essence of the company. The result? A set of

core values, defined by IBMers for IBMers, that shape the way we lead, the way we decide, and the way we act.

Here is the way IBM's own website describes this important organizational innovation:

> In that regard, IBM's jams represent a new form of organizational intervention, a way to accelerate change. As their name suggests, these jams are like jazz improvisations, connecting people who might otherwise never meet, allowing them to formulate and build on each other's thoughts, and in the process, create something entirely new. Because they are radically open and democratic—everybody has the same capacity to participate, regardless of level or expertise—jams speak to the expectations of today's professional worker.

In 2006, several years after that ValuesJam at IBM, then-CEO Sam Palmisano sponsored an "IBM InnovationJam®" that was by far the largest brainstorming conversation ever held up to that time. Patterned after the 2003 event, it took place over the course of two seventy-two-hour time periods. It included over 150,000 participants, from sixty-seven companies in one hundred four countries, and it produced a powerful set of ideas for new businesses and new products.

A core group of IBM staff sifted through the thousands of ideas, boiled them to down to a manageable number of possibilities, and launched the second round of brainstorming.

That 2006 event ultimately led to a $100 million investment by IBM in ten separate new ventures, most of which were major financial and strategic successes.

And although I do not have any inside information from IBM, I have to believe that the InnovationJam® accomplished much more for IBM than just those new products and their revenue streams.

Just imagine what it must have felt like to IBM employees to be listened to, and to have had their ideas taken seriously by the company's senior executives. Even if your particular suggestion didn't make the cut, it must have been incredibly confirming—to say nothing of engaging—to be able to participate in a process that became so critical to IBM's future success.

Organizational Jams essentially leverage social media technology to create massive extended conversations. Those conversations, which in some ways resemble the discussion threads that are so common among popular social media services like Facebook and LinkedIn, enable large numbers of employees to collaborate virtually as they confront tough problems, identify new product opportunities, and even design entirely new business ventures.

Looking Ahead

I know this is an incomplete survey of innovative approaches for creating extraordinary meetings. My goal has simply been to open your eyes to what's possible when you are willing to experiment with new ways of including more smart people in problem-solving conversations. Please use these examples and stories as stimulus to your own creativity. Be willing to break out of the box, and to try one of these approaches or your own variation.

At this point I have two more requests. First, while I will be personally gratified if you transform the way you plan and lead your own meetings, I won't be fully satisfied until you take the next step and work on building a deep organizational culture that values collaborative leadership and makes all its meetings matter. That's my focus in Chapter Eight.

Second, I want you to join me in a look ahead: where do we go from here? That's a question I can't actually answer on my own, so in the Afterword I invite you to join me in an ongoing conversation that goes well beyond this book—an online discussion forum where together we can share our stories, trade insights, and engage in a continuing conversation about leading meeting that matter.

I intend to make the book's website (www.makingmeetingsmatter. com) a dynamic, open forum about corporate conversations— and a vehicle for achieving my goal of shifting corporate cultures in the direction of more collaboration, wider power-sharing, more excitement, and ultimately a dramatic increase in both organizational performance and individual engagement.

Chapter Eight

BUILDING A CONSTRUCTIVE CONVERSATIONAL CULTURE

Let's come up for air now as we reflect together on what we've learned and where we can go from here. In this chapter I want to step back, reflect on the ideas we've explored together, offer some broader perspectives on what constitutes a successful meeting and suggest how you can create a constructive organizational culture that embraces conversation as the foundation of work in the digital age.

Let's revisit my opening call for a collaborative leadership mindset and consider a final set of *New Rules*—principles that you can follow to lead your team, and the organization as a whole, towards a shared mindset that:

- Views meetings as opportunities for conversation, learning, and consensus-building.

- Recognizes that in the age of networked knowledge no one alone is smarter than everyone together.

- Values diversity and seeks new perspectives, particularly about old, long-standing challenges.

- Sees leadership as a way to engage staff and learn from them.

- Builds power by sharing it.

- Believes in collaboration and the power of brainstorming.

- Respects individuals as complex human beings with personal lives and relationships that extend far beyond the organization's boundaries.

- Believes that people want to contribute, to be successful, and to feel valued and respected.

That may seem idealistic, but I can tell you that the most well-respected organizations in the world, those who regularly appear on the best-place-to-work lists, operate with that kind of mindset.

If you buy into the notion of a conversational, collaborative mindset, then the core question becomes, "How can you create an organizational culture that practices those values?"

While I don't have any magic feather that can transform your organization (or you) overnight, I do have some thoughts about how your behavior as a leader can begin to move others in the right direction.

That's what this final chapter is about.

The Mindset of a Change Leader

The best definition I've ever heard of effective leadership goes something like this:

> A good leader doesn't make people do what he (or she) wants; a good leader makes others want what the leader wants.

In other words, leadership is about engaging people's hearts even more than their minds. If your staff shares your vision of what's possible, understands why what's possible is desirable, and shares your desire to make that vision come alive, they'll do what they need to do to make it happen. Show them the future, share your passion about the journey, and get out of their way (but stay close by in case they need coaching or advice).

That all sounds good. But in my experience that's only the beginning. As the old saying goes, you can't push a string. Leadership means being first among equals, not being a dictator or a policeman. The challenge facing any leader is how to create that strong desire in your staff for the same kinds of outcomes that you want.

I rely on a three-step process for leading organizational change that may help you overcome that challenge. It's relatively simple, but it includes three more New Rules for thinking through the journey that you want to take:

- Dream your destination

- Design with data

- Discover by doing

Here, briefly, is what each of these three New Rules means.

NEW RULE: Dream your destination

Stephen Covey advised us to "Start with the end in mind." But I don't think that is enough. Yes, it makes all kinds of sense to be clear about where you are trying to go, or what kind of organizational culture you want to create. For me, that way of thinking about your task is necessary but not sufficient; it feels too analytic, emotionless, and left-brained.

That's why I start with Dreaming. A dream, in contrast to a plan, suggests a vision that is ambitious, inspirational, and even audacious.

When Steve Jobs first launched Apple Computer out of a garage in Palo Alto, he was already talking about changing the world. He wasn't satisfied with building a functional personal computer. From the very beginning he wanted to create technology that was "cool"—and that was completely different from anything that already existed.

Remember that when Jobs first introduced the iPod he didn't get on stage and talk about the hard drive's megabit capacity. No, his first statement was that he had "a thousand songs in my pocket."

That's a dream—every bit as audacious in its own way as Martin Luther King's "I Have a Dream" speech. Like King, Jobs touched people's emotions; in his case it was their desire to have something new, powerful, and "cool." That day, he made his audience—and consumers worldwide—want what he wanted: a pocketful of pleasure (and personal convenience and control—the ability to listen to whatever song you want to listen to, when you want to, and at a very low price).

To summarize, "Dream Your Destination" calls for an explicit vision accompanied by strong, ambitious desire. Be clear about the destination, but focus on its emotional appeal.

I would add one other ingredient when you begin sharing that dream. Include clear statements about *why* the dream is desirable, *why* it is important, and *why* it is worth pursuing.

Simon Sinek's book *Start with Why* reminds us that "Why?" is by far the most compelling question of all; knowing *why* something is important is far more inspiring and motivating than simply knowing *what* a vision or goal is, or *how* it will change experiences.

NEW RULE: Design with data

Now, as you actually begin the journey to that destination you are dreaming about (a corporate culture that values conversations and treats them as central to success), it's time to be realistic, and to base that journey on an accurate understanding of where you are and what the pathway to the future will be like.

It is impossible for me to offer generic, one-size-fits-all advice for this part of your journey. However, there are several broad rules about leading constructive change that do make sense across many different situations.

NEW RULE: Know where you are before you start the journey

As my good friend and former colleague Bruce Rogow is fond of saying, "If you want to fly to Los Angeles it makes a great deal of difference whether you are starting in New York City or Honolulu."

To apply that rule more specifically, gather some facts and opinions about how productive, or non-productive, your meetings are now. Ask basic questions like these:

- Are the meetings well-attended? Do invitees frequently have reasons for missing regular meetings? What are the reasons they don't participate?

- How do participants feel about the meetings? Do they find them worthwhile, or a waste of time?

- Do your meetings start and end on time? Or do you have to wait for participants to show up?

- Do participants understand each meeting's purpose and objectives? Are those objectives met when the meetings conclude?

- Do participants have a clear and common understanding of what decisions were reached during the meeting (if reaching decisions was a goal)? Does everyone know who is responsible for implementing those decisions?

- Are the meetings characterized by free-wheeling, open conversations, or do you have difficulty getting anyone to talk? Do a small number of people dominate the conversation?

- How serious are these issues? Do you need a complete overhaul of your meeting practices, or will a few minor tweaks produce the improvement you are seeking?

It's hard for people to get excited about a vague future. So when you talk about your vision, be specific. Describe it in terms of your desire for meetings that everyone enjoys, for conversations that are engaging, enlightening, and fun. Ask your staff what kind of meetings they would enjoy, and add their ideas to your leadership vocabulary. Paint pictures of a future that your staff can see themselves experiencing.

NEW RULE: Numbers are data, but so are stories

Remember Alice Dee's description back in Chapter 2 of how meetings at Odyssey Enterprises are far more focused on stories than they are on numbers? One of the best ways to gain a deep understanding of the current situation is to ask people to tell you stories about meetings they've liked and meetings they haven't liked. Themes emerging from a collection of stories will paint a much clearer picture of where your meeting issues and challenges are than pages of quantitative tables and charts.

As you are collecting and listening to those stories, however, be sure to determine if they are based on objective, verifiable observations and not on experience-free myths. For example, that high-tech CEO who wanted all of her staff in the office every day actually believed that they were close by; it wasn't until she walked through the corporate facility with us that she realized she was out of touch with reality. She was preparing to embark on a journey without knowing where she was starting from.

NEW RULE: Don't do it alone

Leaders don't exist without followers. But this rule isn't about finding followers; it's about attracting collaborators. When you are beginning to plan out a journey of change it's often difficult to remember that there is incredible power in the wisdom of the crowd. Go back and reread Chapter 1, and remember that no one person—including you—has all the answers. If the change process is a journey, it's a group tour.

Share your early thoughts about what a conversational culture could be like, and how it would feel. But use those ideas as conversation starters—as themes that invite your staff to share their own ideas and contribute to the emerging vision.

In essence, the way to build a conversational culture is to live a conversational life.

Which brings us directly to my third broad principle:

NEW RULE: Discover by doing

This is another way of saying that we learn through experience. As I mentioned in Chapter 2, I didn't invent this principle but I do believe in it:

> It's easier to act your way into a new kind of thinking than it is to think your way into a new kind of acting.

The best way to build a conversational culture is to lead as if you already have one.

In *The Fifth Age of Work*, Andrew Jones emphasizes the importance of innovation and creativity in today's economy, highlighting in particular the role that co-working facilities have played in putting freelancers, entrepreneurs, telecommuters and other "free agents" side by side in shared workplaces. Jones, like me, sees the collision of ideas that results from co-working as central to what he calls a "culture of experimentation."

He also describes how companies like Google, 3M, W.L. Gore Associates, and even larger more established organizations like IBM, Procter & Gamble, and even AT&T are driving new product development, creating entirely new businesses, and redesigning the way they operate internally—all as a result of embracing a mindset that values experimentation and encourages candid conversations up, down, and all around their organizations.

I'm calling for that kind of mindset—discovering by doing—as the most effective way to lead organizational change. If you want to create a conversational culture, don't just talk about it, or rely on making a compelling business case.

Just do it.

Start today to lead your meetings and other corporate conversations as if the other participants have good ideas that you want to hear about.

As I have already noted, discovering by doing means learning from experience. It means being willing to try something even when you are not certain it will work.

There is an old story (I really don't remember where I first heard it) that in IBM's very early days a young project manager had the unpleasant task of informing IBM's founder and CEO John Watson Sr. that a major design initiative had gotten off track and had to be shut down after costing the company about $6 million.

When he finished explaining what had happened, the project manager said to Watson, "I'm sorry that I screwed up. I suppose you'll be wanting my resignation."

To which Watson supposedly replied:

> Hell no! I just paid your tuition. I don't want you taking what you've just learned anywhere else.

That's what I mean by a culture of experimentation. Not everything you try is going to work at first, but if you are convinced that collaborative conversations are important, then start leading meetings that are based on the New Rules I've described throughout this book. It may take some time—and it might take longer than you want it to—but if you begin acting like a conversational leader, you will soon find yourself living in a conversational culture.

What Kind of Leadership Style Should you Employ?

When someone asks me what leadership style or approach is most effective, the only legitimate answer I can offer is, "It depends." But of course the next question is always, "Depends on what?"

That question has probably driven more research and PhD dissertations than any other issue in the field of management.

And the best answer to the question that I know of comes from a landmark study conducted almost fifty years ago by Ken Blanchard (yes, that Ken Blanchard, he of *The One-Minute Manager* fame) and Paul Hersey.

Their research, and the Situational Leadership model they developed, was first published in 1977 in a book called *Management of Organizational Behavior* (now in its ninth edition, with Dewey Johnson as a third author).

I believe the so-called Hersey-Blanchard model of situational leadership remains incredibly powerful and relevant today.

The Hersey-Blanchard leadership model is simple in concept, but deeply complex in application. The logic goes like this: when a team (or a single individual) is faced with a particular task, the most important factor is how capable or experienced the team is with that task.

If a team is new to a task, it usually needs directive, structured leadership to be successful. In contrast, if the team members are experienced and fully capable of handling the challenge, then a "hands-off" or delegating style of leadership is generally more effective.

That may seem like common sense, but the history of leadership is filled with examples of leaders who had only one dominant style and applied it to every team, in every imaginable situation.

Adjusting Your Leadership Style to the Situation

The toughest challenge for any leader is to determine how much, and what kind, of formal task-oriented direction is right for a given team facing a particular task. Moreover, as a team gains experience it typically becomes more capable over time, so an effective leader must be able to "back off" as the team's competence grows relative to the task.

It's also worth remembering that backing off – releasing control and direction through delegation – is far easier, and more acceptable to most people, than tightening up. When a leader has been relatively loose and easy-going, team members usually resent having increased control imposed on them (even when they need it). They typically believe, rightly or wrongly, that they have learned how to get the job done and they don't like being told how to do something they think they have already mastered.

> The Hersey-Blanchard model focuses on two key dimensions of a work situation, and then suggests four prototypical leadership styles.

The two key factors that define a leadership challenge are (1) the nature of the task; and (2) the experience, or the maturity, of the team members relative to that task.

A task can be routine and well-understood, or it can be problematic, require creativity, or even be a "wicked problem."

Team Maturity

A team may have lots of experience with a routine task, or even with confronting wicked problems. Or the team could be newly formed, with inexperienced members who need basic instruction and hand-holding for even a relatively simple, routine task. The Situational Leadership model describes four levels of team maturity and mindset:

- Unable and insecure (needing handholding, reassurance, instruction, and patience)

- Unable but willing (needing and wanting direction/instruction to be successful)

- Capable but unwilling (requiring motivational leadership if not formal direction)

- Very capable and confident (calling for "hands-off" delegation)

Four Leadership Styles

The interaction of team maturity and task requirements then points towards one of four basic leadership styles:

- **Directing**—providing clear direction and "how-to" instruction

- **Coaching**—more teaching, persuading, and motivating

- **Supporting**—sharing in the planning conversation and focusing more on relationships than on the task itself

- **Delegating**—overseeing the team but staying in the background; monitoring progress and offering feedback as needed

I particularly like the notion of an evolution in leadership style as a team builds experience/maturity and confidence/commitment for any particular task. Note that the starting point for an evolving leadership style that begins with a new task and an inexperienced team (relative to a particular task) is Directing – providing clear direction and formal instruction to help the team master its challenges.

Then as the team members grow in capability their leader can "back off" and operate more as a Coach, continuing to teach and guide, but with a lighter touch and more of a motivational role.

As the team continues to improve over time the leader can step further back into a Supporting role, treating the members more like peers, giving them more discretion, and paying more attention to their working relationshps than their task responsibilities.

Finally, when it is clear that team is fully competent and achieving its goals, the leader becomes a Delegator, staying in the background, monitoring progress, and praising the members for their accomplishments.

So as you begin the journey of developing a conversational culture, start with a compelling vision (Dream your Destination), assess your team's readiness, or maturity, for the journey (Design with Data), and then begin the journey and adapt along the way based on your sense of progress and on the team's mastery of the values and behaviors that achieve your vision (Discover by Doing).

A Final Thought: How Do You Know a Meeting's Been Successful?

This question came up during one of my research interviews, and I've been pondering it for some time. At one level the answer is straightforward; it depends on how well, and how completely, the meeting achieved your initial purpose. If you set a goal of reaching a group decision, or designing a new marketing campaign, or resolving a budget conflict, and you achieve that purpose, then it's easy to say the meeting was successful.

Or was it? Like all other human experience, meetings have multiple outcomes and consequences, and the quality of the group's decision—or invention, or problem resolution—may not meet your expectations, even it was adequate for the situation. More importantly, you may have made progress even if you didn't achieve your ultimate goal.

Even if on the surface the group failed to complete its task, it is worth remembering that the participants may have forged new relationships, learned important facts about the issue or each other, or generated new ideas that will eventually produce even more meaningful results.

In other words, determining whether (and how) a particular meeting mattered is complicated. I find it helpful to assess my own meeting experiences in four specific ways:

- **Was the meeting *efficient*?** Was the time well spent? Did the meeting include only those people who needed to be part of the decision, or of the process that produced that decision? Did the meeting last only as long as was needed?

- **Did the meeting achieve its primary purpose?** How close did you come to resolving the issues that led to the meeting in the first place? Is there clarity about the decision, or the problem resolution? Do the participants understand what will happen next as a result of the meeting, and—most importantly—does everyone understand who will do what by when? In other words, is there clear accountability for carrying out the actions that were agreed on?

- **Did the meeting enhance the participants' capability for future actions?** Every meeting is a step on a journey towards enhanced team maturity, or capability. Even if you weren't able to resolve a pressing problem, if you made progress and improved the working relationships among the participants, you should consider the meeting at least a partial success.

- **How do the participants *feel* about the meeting?** Admittedly, this is a purely subjective dimension, but the collective wisdom of the meeting participants is a powerful indicator of how effective the meeting experience was for them.

Back in Chapter Four I described the practice of an After-Action Review (or AAR). I said there, and it bears repeating, that it is unrealistic to hold a formal AAR following every meeting; but spending the last five minutes of a meeting leading a group debriefing on how the meeting went and how it could have been improved is an important part of building a long-term corporate culture that values constructive conversations.

As I have already noted, Jim Horan likes to end his meetings with a simple but powerful question to all the other participants: "What will you do differently as a result of this conversation?" If the answer is "Nothing" then you have to wonder if the time and energy that went into the meeting could have been spent more effectively doing something else

Looking Ahead

Just as there is no one-size-fits-all formula for leadership, there is no universal rule for leading meetings that matter, or for building a conversational culture. However, I hope you've found the advice and the rules and tools I've shared throughout this book useful.

Ultimately, transforming corporate conversations is something you have to want so much that you are ready to try the New Rules even if you are not sure how to implement them. As I've said so many times throughout the book, success is much more a matter of adopting a new mindset and learning by doing than it is about perfecting new skills.

If I've been successful I have persuaded you that it's worth the risk. If you want to live and work in a collaborative, respectful, and high-performing organization as much as I do—and have some specific ideas about how to do that—then I have accomplished my objective.

Thank you for sticking with me through this journey. What's ahead is a brief request that you join me in a continuing and extended conversation about meetings and how to make them more effective. I have already set up a website (www.makingmeetingsmatter.com) and a forum where we can share experiences, explore what works and what doesn't, and build a community of committed conversational leaders. I hope you'll want to keep learning and growing as much as I do. Please feel free to contact me any time at jim@makingmeetingsmatter.com with questions, comments, and your own stories about meetings.

Afterword

CONTINUING THE CONVERSATION

I have to admit that I find it more than mildly ironic to be writing a book about conversations. A book is essentially a lengthy, one-way communication, whereas a conversation in its most meaningful form is a real-time, interactive, and highly engaging experience that connects two or more people with each other in deep personal ways.

In a conversation each participant listens in real time to a speaker, whose "speeches" are typically kept under a minute or two, stopping to think but more importantly to listen to the other participants—to get immediate feedback and to hear other ideas—sometimes supporting, sometimes challenging—on the same general subject.

In contrast, a book is a collection of ideas, insights, and meaning produced by one person (in this case, me) in the hope that others, like you, will read them and somehow be changed.

I am writing these words sitting at my workstation, all alone, on an unusual rainy afternoon in northern California. You are reading them sometime much later, somewhere far away. I don't know who you are, where you are, or what my ideas mean to you.

But I want these words, as one-sided as a book makes them, to feel as much like a conversation as possible; I've done my best to write conversationally, not formally. I am imagining that you are sitting across the room from me, nodding at some of my comments, and shaking your head at others. Every once in a while you think to yourself "What does he mean by that?" or "Boy, does that story resonate with my experience."

But because we are separated in time and space you can't respond directly, or ask me to repeat an idea you don't understand. So this hasn't been a "real" conversation, in the way it would be if we were sitting across from each other, with a beer or a cup of tea at hand and a jazz band playing in the background (I'm trying to conjure up in your mind an image of a coffee house, or a local brew pub, or a college student union—those are the kinds of places where many of the most meaningful conversations take place).

Notice however that I didn't try to place us in a conference room at the office. Many if not most workplace meetings do take place in conference rooms, but we know that all too often those conversations, which may or may not be important, are boring, mundane, and meaningless.

My goal is this book has been to engage you in a virtual conversation about "real" conversations—what makes them good when they are good, and why good conversations are so elusive. If I have been successful, you are now energized, engaged, and convinced that you can make your own work-related conversations more meaningful, and more fun to be part of.

Now that the book is complete I want to have real-time conversations with many of you who have taken this journey with me. I have already launched a website (www. makingmeetingsmatter.com) where we can exchange ideas in real time, holding an extended, asynchronous conversation through an open online discussion group.

I also intend to host periodic open-ended conference calls where you will be welcome to raise questions, offer opinions, and exchange ideas, insights, and meaning. I'd love to hear your stories about great meetings, and about awful ones too. What can we learn together from our experiences? Check the book's website for a current schedule of open conversations.

I've been on a learning journey about corporate meetings and other conversations for many years (I hesitate to call it "research," because that makes it sound so formal and even academic). And I learn best from other people, from listening to their experiences, their ideas, and most of all the meanings they create out of those experiences.

As I sat down several months ago to begin putting this book together I realized that although I have a wealth of personal experiences that I want to share, I am only one person with limited experience. Thus, many of the stories, insights, and guiding principles that you have read about here came from conversations I've had with friends, colleagues, and experts of all kinds.

I've identified many of my teachers and mentors (both formal and informal) in the Acknowledgements section, but here I just want to assure you that my journey isn't over—and I hope yours isn't either. Please connect with me at www.makingmeetingsmatter.com and join the ongoing public and private conversations I'm having about conversations at work and making meetings matter.

RESOURCES AND NOTES

I've deliberately avoided using footnotes to make your reading experience simpler and less confusing. However, this Resource Guide identifies most of the books, websites, and other sources I have mentioned—chapter by chapter.

Links to most of them are "live" in the digital versions of the book. I have grouped the resources mentioned specifically in the book by chapter; following those lists I have added a number of additional sources that I have found useful.

INTRODUCTION

"Conversation is at the very heart of knowledge-based work." —Alan Webber, "What's So New About the New Economy?" *Harvard Business Review*, January-February, 1993. Reprint #93109.

"Nobody is smarter than everybody."—Rod Collins, *Leadership in a Wiki World: Leveraging Collective Knowledge to Make the Leap to Extraordinary Performance*. Indianapolis, Indiana: Dog Ear Publishing, 2010.

We shape our tools and then our tools shape us. https://mcluhangalaxy.wordpress.com/2013/04/01/we-shape-our-tools-and-thereafter-our-tools-shape-us/

CHAPTER ONE

State of the Global Workplace Report 2013—The Gallup Organization. http://www.gallup.com/services/178517/state-global-workplace.aspx

You could lose 90 percent of your staff as the economy improves—Right Management survey (http://www.right.com/wps/wcm/connect/right-us-en/home/thoughtwire/categories/media-center/Most+Employees+Plan+to+Pursue+New+Job+Opportunities+in+2014+Reveals+Right+Management+Poll). Accessed September 8, 2015.

Three basic changes in information access and personal communications. I first heard this way of describing the impact of digital technologies and the Internet at the 2013 annual conference of the National Speakers Association in Philadelphia. It came from a then nineteen-year-old German named Philipp Riederle; he had already been blogging for more than five years and had become globally famous as an iPhone expert.

I have since had many conversations with colleagues and clients about what it means to be so globally interconnected, so the way I express the phenomenon today is my own, but I do want to acknowledge Herr Riederle's contribution to my thinking.

The way we work has changed. There are many books that make this assertion; here are a few that I am familiar with and find insightful:

Blades, Joan, and Nanette Fondas. *The Custom-Fit Workplace*. San Francisco: Jossey-Bass, 2010.

Clow, Julie. *The Work Revolution*. Hoboken, NJ: John Wiley & Sons, 2012.

Gratton, Lynda. *The Shift*. London: Harper-Collins, 2011.

Howe, Neil, and William Straus. *The Fourth Turning*. New York: Broadway Books, 1997.

Huptic, Vladke. *The Management Shift*. London: Palgrave McMillan, 2014.

Jones, Andrew. *The Fifth Age of Work*. Portland, OR: Night Owls Press, 2013.

Miller, Paul. *The Digital Workplace*. London: TECL Publishing, 2012.

Ressler, Cali, and Jody Thompson. *Why Work Sucks and How to Fix It*. New York: The Penguin Group, 2010.

Ross, Ruth. *Coming Alive: The Journey to Reengage Your Life and Your Career*. Sacramento: Authority Publishing, 2014.

Taylor, William C., and Polly Labore. *Mavericks at Work*. New York: William Morrow, 2006.

Webb, Maynard, and Carlye Adler. *Rebooting Work*. San Francisco: Jossey-Bass, 2013.

CHAPTER TWO
How many business meetings are held each day?

"11 million meetings a day" pops up all over the Internet; a Google search on "How many business meetings are held each day?" generates over 265,000 results (in less than one second). In all honesty, I only reviewed the top dozen or so.

As nearly as I can tell the most frequently cited source for that 11 million number comes from a 1998 white paper published by MCI Communications (now Verizon) titled "Meetings in America: A study of trends, costs, and attitudes toward business travel and teleconferencing, and their impact on productivity." That paper includes the following sentence: "Meetings dominate business life in America today. According to the National Statistics Council, 37 percent of employee time is spent in meetings. *Other data indicate there are 11 million business meetings each and every day*." [emphasis added]

Unfortunately the MCI paper does not identify any sources for the "other data." But it's also worth noting that the number of meetings has to have gone up substantially in the last seventeen years. Just consider how many more conference calls and distributed meetings there are, let alone the growth in our general propensity for group conversations and collaborative efforts of all kinds. Nevertheless, I have relied on the 11 million meetings a day estimate while knowing it is a (very) conservative estimate.

The cost of a meeting:

See Rick Gilbert's *Speaking Up: Surviving Executive Presentations* (Berrett-Koehler, San Francisco, 2013) for a compelling analysis of how much a typical meeting costs; he includes the participants' salaries, the cost of the meeting room and associated audio-visual equipment, as well as the preparation time that precedes the meeting.

A few good books on how to lead an effective meeting:

Doyle, Michael, and David Straus. *How to Make Meetings Work.* New York: Berkeley Publishing Group, 1993.

Harvard Business Review. Running Meetings. Boston: *Harvard Business Review* Press, 2014.

Kayser, Thomas A. *Mining Group Gold: How to Cash in on the Collaborative Brain Power of a Group.* El Segundo, CA: Serif Publishing, 1990.

Lencione, Patrick. *Death by Meeting.* San Francisco: Jossey-Bass, 2004.

Lippincott, Sharon M. *Meetings: Do's, Don'ts, and Donuts: The Complete Handbook for Successful Meetings.* Pittsburgh: Lighthouse Point Press, 1999.

Pittampalli, Al. *Read This Before Our Next Meeting: How to Get Things Done.* New York: Portfolio/Penguin, 2015.

Don't hold a meeting if you don't need one:

Schmidt, Eric, and Jonathan Rosenberg. *How Google Works.* New York City: Grand Central Publishing, 2014.

CHAPTER THREE

Athos, Anthony G, and John J. Gabarro. *Interpersonal Behavior: Communication and Understanding in Relationships.* Englewood Cliffs, NJ: Prentice Hall, 1978.

Bregman, Peter. "Employees Can't Be Summed Up by a Personality Test"—*Harvard Business Review* blog, August 19, 2015. https://hbr.org/2015/08/employees-cant-be-summed-up-by-a-personality-test

Buckingham, Marcus, and Donald O. Clifton, PhD, Now Discover Your Strengths. New York: Free Press, 2001.

Clifton, Donald O., and Edward "Chip" Anderson, StrengthsQuest. Washington, DC: The Gallup Organization, 2001-2002.

CoreClarity: http://www.coreclarity.net

CHAPTER FOUR

60 *Minutes* program on Mindfulness:

http://www.cbsnews.com/videos/mindfulness-2/ (accessed October 15, 2015)

Amazon Staff Meetings:

http://conorneill.com/2012/11/30/amazon-staff-meetings-no-powerpoint/

Campbell, Steven. *Making Your Mind Magnificent: Use the New Brain Science to Transform Your Life: End Negative Thinking, Improve Focus and Clarity, and Be Happier*. Rohnert Park, CA: Intelligent Heart Press, 2014.

Kaplan, Abraham. *The Conduct of Inquiry: Methodology for Behavioral Science*. Piscataway, NJ: Transaction Publishers, 1998.

Judith Glaser quote from "Leaders: It's Time to Fix the Way You Listen," *Entrepreneur* Magazine, October 31, 2014 (http://www.entrepreneur.com/article/239221, accessed March 15, 2015)

After-Action Reviews:

The Knowledge Sharing Toolkit wiki website was developed originally by the Global Agricultural Research Partnership (http://www.cgiar.org)

http://www.kstoolkit.org/After+Action+Review (accessed October 15, 2015)

CHAPTER FIVE

"The Place Just Right"

I have discovered that my obscure reference in the chapter title to a popular Quaker song titled "Simple Gifts" is way too vague for most readers. I do want to give credit where it's due. The song includes these lines:

"'Tis the gift to be simple, 'tis the gift to be free;

'Tis the gift to come down to where we ought to be;

And when we find ourselves in the place just right,

'Twill be in the valley of love and delight."

I find that phrasing both haunting and compelling, and it is such an apt description of the feeling we get when a meeting or conversation goes well that I chose to use it as heart of this chapter's title.

Value of seeing the outdoors for well-being:

Ulrich, Roger S. "View Through a Window May Influence Recovery from Surgery." *Science*, v. 224, March, 1984.

Schwartz, Tony, and Christine Porath, "Why You Hate Work," *New York Times*, May, 2014. http://www.nytimes.com/2014/06/01/ opinion/sunday/why-you-hate-work.html?emc=edit_ tnt_20140530&nlid=64161719&tnte-mail0=y&_r=0

CHAPTER SIX

Two thirds of knowledge work takes place outside traditional corporate facilities:

Ware, James P. "The Future of Business Collaboration: A Citrix GoToMeeting Corporate White Paper" (p. 7-8) Available at: http://www.thefutureofwork.net/assets/FOW_FutureofBusiness Collaboration.pdf

Well over 30 million U.S. workers are mobile/flexible:

Ware, James P. "The Future of Business Collaboration: A Citrix GoToMeeting Corporate White Paper" (p. 9) Available at: http://www.thefutureofwork.net/assets/FOW_ FutureofBusinessCollaboration.pdf

Remote work programs can save 40 percent or more of workforce support costs:

Johansen, Bob, and David Sibbet. *Leading Business Teams: How Teams Can Use Technology and Group Process Tools to Enhance Performance.* Boston: Addison-Wesley, 1991.

Ware James P., and Charles E. Grantham, "The Future of Work: Changing patterns of workforce management and their impact on the workplace," *Facility Management Journal*, May 2003.

CHAPTER SEVEN

Scenario Planning

The "bible" for scenario planning is *The Art of the Long View: Planning for the Future in an Uncertain World* (New York: Currency Doubleday, 1996) by Peter Schwartz. The book describes Schwartz's early experiences as a strategic planner at Shell Oil Company. There he and several colleagues, including Arie de Geus and Pierre Wack, developed the scenario planning process for exploring multiple, alternative views of possible futures.

The Art of the Long View: Planning for the Future in an Uncertain World.

If you want to pursue scenario planning in depth, start with *The Art of the Long View*, but also be sure to read these seminal articles from the *Harvard Business Review*:

de Geus, Arie. "Planning as Learning." March 1988. https://hbr.org/1988/03/planning-as-learning

Wack, Pierre. "Scenarios: Uncharted Waters Ahead." September 1985. https://hbr.org/1985/09/scenarios-uncharted-waters-ahead

See also, James P. Ware, "Scenario Planning: Preparing for Uncertainty" in *The New HR Analytics: Predicting the Economic Value of Your Company's Human Capital Investments*, by Dr. Jac Fitz-Enz. New York: Amazon, 2010.

Future Search

See Marvin Weisbord and Sandra Janoff, *Future Search: Getting the Whole System in the Room for Vision, Commitment, and Action*, Third Edition. San Francisco: Berrett-Koehler, 2010.

The World Café

See: *The World Café: Shaping Our Futures Through Conversations that Matter,* by Juanita Brown with David Isaacs and the World Café Community. San Francisco: Berrett-Koehler, 2006.

For current perspectives and continuing conversations about the World Café, visit the World Café community website at: http://www.theworldcafe.com/_

For more information about professional graphic recorders, contact the International Forum of Visual Practitioners, at https://www.ifvp.org/ or The Grove, at http://www.grove.com/

See also these two books by David Sibbet, the founder of the The Grove:

Sibbet, David. *Visual Meetings: How Graphics, Sticky Notes, and Idea Mapping Can Transform Group Productivity.*

Sibbet, David. *Visual Leaders: New Tools for Visioning, Management, and Organizational Change.*

Campbell, Steven. *Making Your Mind Magnificent.* Lake Placid, NY: Aviva Publishing, 2010.

Business Process Redesign

The original source of business process redesign (BPR) ideas and approaches was a *Harvard Business Review* article by the late Michael Hammer:

"Reengineering Work: Don't Automate, Obliterate!" July-August, 1990. https://hbr.org/1990/07/reengineering-work-dont-automate-obliterate

Hammer developed the BPR approach in greater detail, and with many compelling examples, in the book he later co-authored with James Champy, *Reengineering the Corporation: A Manifesto for Business Revolution.* New York: Harperbusiness, 2001.

I had the privilege of working directly with both Jim Champy and the late Mike Hammer in the early 1990s, when I was a Vice President at Index Systems, based in Cambridge, Massachusetts.

Work-Thrus

Work-Thrus were developed by Rod Collins when he was Chief Operating Officer of the Blue Cross Blue Shield Federal Employee Program. For a detailed description of the process and examples of its impact, see Collin's compelling book, *Leadership in a Wiki World: Leveraging Collective Knowledge to Make the Leap to Extraordinary Performance.* Indianapolis: Dog Ear Publishing, 2010.

Organizational Jams

This process of global, inclusive organizational brainstorming and problem-solving has been most effectively used by IBM and ATT. For their public descriptions of the process see the following websites:

IBM's Organizational Jams

See "Our Values: Jobs at IBM," http://www-03.ibm.com/ employment/our_values.html (accessed January 27, 2015)

"A Global Innovation Jam." http://www-03.ibm.com/ibm/history/ ibm100/us/en/icons/innovationjam/ (accessed January 27, 2015)

CHAPTER EIGHT

Sinek, Simon. *Start with Why: How Great Leaders Inspire Everyone to Take Action.* Portfolio Publishing, 2011.

The best sources of ideas and guidelines for successful change leadership come from three books by John Kotter and two by Chip and Dan Heath:

Kotter, John, Holger Rathgeber, and Peter Mueller, *Our Iceberg Is Melting: Changing and Succeeding under Any Conditions.* New York: St. Martin's Press, 2006.

Kotter, John. *Leading Change.* Cambridge, MA: Harvard Business Review Press, 2012.

Kotter, John. *Accelerate: Building Strategic Agility for a Faster-*

Moving World. Cambridge, MA: *Harvard Business Review* Press, 2014.

Heath, Chip, and Dan Heath, *Made to Stick: Why Some Ideas Survive and Others Die*. Random House, 2007.

Heath, Chip, and Dan Heath, *Switch: How to Change Things When Change is Hard*. New York: Broadway Books, 2010.

Jones, Andrew. *The Fifth Age of Work: How Companies Can Redesign Work to Become More Innovative in a Cloud Economy*. Portland, OR: Night Owls Press, 2013.

The Situational Leadership model developed by Hersey and Blanchard was first published in 1977 in a book called *Management of Organizational Behavior* (now in its 9th edition, with Dewey Johnson as a third author).

Hersey, Paul, Kenneth H. Blanchard, and Dewey E. Johnson, *Management of Organizational Behavior: Leading Human Resources* (Ninth Edition). New York: Prentice Hall, 2007.

ACKNOWLEDGEMENTS

Writing is both an exceptionally lonely and a massively collaborative activity. The first thing any writer learns is to sit at the keyboard alone—and to do it over and over again, day after day, converting ideas into written words.

However, for me at least, most of those ideas developed out of conversations with other people. Yes, some of what I've written emerged from personal introspection and interpretation, but I can always trace my best ideas back to conversations with friends and colleagues, and sometimes even with strangers.

This book is no exception. I would never have started, let alone finished, this journey if I were living alone. I have to begin by thanking Cindy, my wife, my best friend, and my biggest fan for the last forty-eight years. She believed in me from the beginning, long before I believed in myself.

Cindy's willingness to tolerate my long hours, late nights, many business trips away from home, and all-too-frequent stubbornness for so many years continues to astound me. She is a consummate and patient listener whose astute questions and observations have contributed profoundly to my growing understanding of how to engage in conversations that matter.

There are two other women who also contributed more to this book than they realize, not only by believing in my message but also by serving as sounding boards, accountability partners, and good friends. Cathy Fyock, my writing coach, showed me how to translate my crude ideas about corporate meetings into a logical framework. More importantly, she held my feet to the fire, taught me how to make writing a daily part of my life, and reassured me when I was convinced I was lost, mired in trivia, or stating the obvious.

And Candace Fitzpatrick, who is writing an important business and personal story of her own, is a long-time friend who has become a weekly conversation partner and a wonderful source of new insights about meetings, working relationships, and individual talents. Even though Candace and I live over a thousand miles and two time zones apart, we usually speak with each other once or twice a week, and often several times a day, about our parallel writing projects as well as our lives, spouses, friends, families, and holidays.

I would never have been able to complete this journey without you three women. Thank you, each of you, for your support, your encouragement, and your unwillingness to let me off the hook.

I also want to thank my many other friends and colleagues who helped me make sense of corporate conversations by sharing their own stories, by teaching me about leadership and collaboration, and by challenging my early ideas. I learned how to think about meetings that matter by listening to you.

The following list of other thought partners is long, and certainly incomplete, but I want to begin by acknowledging these storytellers who have generously shared their lessons with me, and with you: Sue Bingham, David Coleman, Diane Coles-Levine, Rod Collins, Benay Dara-Abrams, Alice Dee, David Isaacs, Mark Parcell, Bill Sanders, Patt Schwab, and Gloria Young.

A small part of our son CJ's life story is included in Chapter One. Over the years he and our daughter Wendy have taught Cindy and me a great deal about values, integrity, and collaborative leadership. Each in their own field—he in small business and she in the corporate world—has mastered the art of leading meetings that matter. You two never cease to impress your very proud parents; your wisdom is all over this book, whether you can see it or not.

I also want to thank many other friends and colleagues who generously shared their time and their insights about corporate conversations and leadership with me. Thank you Jack Allen, Joan Blades, Marcus Bowen, Paul Carder, Gaylene Domer, Mark Ellis, Doug Kirkpatrick, Charlie Grantham, Jim Horan, Chris Hood, Bill Jensen, Mike Johnson, Matt Landes, Brady Mick, Mike Moss, Kent Reyling, Bruce Rogow, Ruth Ross, David Shaw, Eric Sineath, Jeff Smithson, Peter Thomson, Mike Wagner, the twenty-five members of my once-a-month no-holds-barred "Talking About Tomorrow" conversation series, and my many friends and mentors in the National Speakers Association. I have learned so much from each of you, and I want you to know how much I appreciate your thoughtfulness and your generosity.

A famous violinist was once asked how long it had taken him to master a particularly difficult piece of music. His reply was instructive: "Six months to learn the notes, and thirty years to make them worth listening to." I feel that way right now. It's taken me a little over a year to finish this book, but a lifetime to learn the "New Rules" I've described here. They have evolved over many years of participating in thousands of meetings, leading many of them myself, and struggling to make sense out of those experiences, both good and bad.

Recognizing how long it took me to get here, I also want to pay tribute to several of my most important mentors and teachers, along with a few very smart people who certainly have no idea how much influence they have had on me.

First, several people I was fortunate enough to work closely with and for: Jim Zamrazil and John Shafer, my first two mentors at Scott, Foresman and Company, who provided me with exceptional advice wrapped around deep caring about my professional development; Karl Weick, a member of my doctoral committee at Cornell, whose creative observations about people, groups, and life in general have had a lasting impact on my understanding of human behavior; and Jack Gabarro, an exceptionally caring senior professor at Harvard Business School who took a fledgling assistant professor under his wing and generously shared both his time and his wisdom.

I also want to acknowledge some of the many brilliant people whose ideas I have absorbed from a distance (although I've had the good fortune to meet, exchange ideas, and even work directly with several of them). Thank you Judy Bardwick, Ken Blanchard, Stephen Campbell, Jim Champy, Peter Drucker, Carolyn Dweck, Rick Gilbert, Judith Glaser, Michael Hammer, Bob Johansen, John Kotter, David Sibbet, Don Tapscott, Alvin Toffler, and Alan Webber. Each of you, whether you know it or not, has made a significant difference in my understanding of what makes meetings matter.

Alan Webber's 1993 *Harvard Business Review* article, "What's So New About the New Economy?" started me down the specific path that led to this book; but I've been influenced, guided, and inspired by every one of these exceptional individuals.

Finally, I've recently discovered that the most enjoyable part of producing a book comes after you submit your initial draft to your editor and publisher. Working with Henry and Devin DeVries and their team at Indie Books International has been both an honor and a pleasure. Thank you for converting my raw ideas into this beautiful book. You've made it feasible for me to share my experiences and perspectives with the whole world in a way that I could never have accomplished on my own.

Thank you all. You and your insights have become an integral part of who I am and how I view the world today; this book is unquestionably a product of mass collaboration.

ABOUT THE AUTHOR

Jim Ware, PhD

Jim Ware, PhD, is a former Harvard Business School professor who has invested his entire career in understanding what organizations must do to thrive in a rapidly changing world.

His business wisdom comes from deep academic knowledge and over thirty years of hands-on experience as a senior executive and a change leader driving corporate innovation. All that work in the trenches taught him how critical meetings are to organizational success and how rare it is for them to be productive, let alone popular.

Jim is the founder and executive director of Making Meetings Matter, a research and advisory firm; and the global research director for Occupiers Journal Limited, publisher of Work & Place. He has co-authored and contributed to several books about the digital economy and its implications for leadership and organizational success.

Today Jim works with professionals like you to turn those dull, boring meetings into highly engaging conversations. A passionate meeting design strategist, he has distilled decades of personal learning into an essential set of "new rules" for designing and leading meetings that matter.

He holds PhD, M.A., and B.Sc. degrees from Cornell University and an MBA (With Distinction) from the Harvard Business School. Jim is an avid skier and a struggling golfer; he lives and works in northern California.

You can reach Jim through the website www. makingmeetingsmatter.com, or email him directly at jim@ makingmeetingsmatter.com.